PETER SELLERS

PETER SELLERS

Derek Sylvester

Proteus London & New York

PROTEUS BOOKS is an imprint of
The Proteus Publishing Group

United States
PROTEUS PUBLISHING CO., INC.
733 Third Avenue
New York, N.Y. 10017
distributed by:
THE SCRIBNER BOOK COMPANIES, INC.
597, Fifth Avenue
New York, N.Y. 10017

United Kingdom
PROTEUS (PUBLISHING) LIMITED
Bremar House,
Sale Place,
London, W2 1PT.

ISBN 0 906071 57 7 (p/b)
      0 906071 51 8 (h/b)

First published in US 1981
First published in UK 1981
© 1981 Derek Sylvester and The Proteus Publishing Group
All rights reserved.

Printed in Great Britain by
Jolly & Barber Ltd., Rugby,
bound by William Brendon & Son Ltd., Tiptree, Essex

PICTURE CREDITS
The Kobal Collection
United Artists
Columbia Pictures
The Rank Organisation
British Lion
ICC
MGM
Warner Bros
Twentieth Century Fox
BBC Picture Library
Radio Times/Hulton Picture L
Syndicated National
Rex Features
Camera Press
Keystone
Sygma
The Sun Newspapers

BOOK SOURCES
TRUE BRITT – by Britt Ekland
   (Sphere 1979)
LOLITA – by Vladimir Nabako
   (Weidenfeld & Nicolson 195

Designed by Tony Kitzinger

Contents

Preface

PETER SELLERS died on July 24 1980 at the age of 55. There are actors – not necessarily the greatest – whose deaths inspire in quite ordinary people an impression of personal bereavement. During his lifetime, the odds seemed powerfully stacked against Sellers ever belonging in that desirable category. He had appeared in too many execrable movies. His tantrums on the set, hiring and firing fellow performers and directors at will, had been too well-publicized. Above all, he had been totally devoid of that indefinable aura out of which cinematic myths are manufactured (a failing that made his premature death, unlike Monroe's or James Dean's, meaningless as movie iconography). His undoubted talents had even been judged incompatible with their chosen medium of expression. In a rather ungenerous entry on the actor in his movie dictionary, critic David Thomson wrote of cinema 'flinching from mimicry and peeling away bogusness'. True enough, except that an unbridled cult of personality over verifiable acting ability tends to reduce some Hollywood movies to the level of talk shows with plots.

Yet when he died, when the tributes poured in and the reminiscences poured out – an ex-valet selling his memoirs to a Sunday tabloid and his favorite clairvoyant interviewing him from beyond the grave – one could detect behind all the tinselly mourning a genuine melancholy, a real sense of loss. Someone once said that the prospect of death "concentrates the mind wonderfully". But this also applies to those who are left behind. Suddenly Sellers the much-married playboy, the temperamental movie star faded to reveal a more endearing Sellers: the Goon, the comic genius who for over twenty years had conjured up a whole gallery of incisive caricatures.

In Hollywood, they say an actor is "only as good as his last picture". By that cruel standard, Sellers was sometimes pretty bad. But when an actor dies, we can forget the Hollywood credo and get his career back into perspective. Which, in Sellers' case, is just as well, as *his* last picture was *The Fiendish Plot of Dr. Fu Manchu*. We begin to be nostalgic about Bloodnok and Bluebottle from *The Goon Show*, union representative Fred Kite, that entrant for the Kissinger look-alike stakes, Dr. Strangelove, and Chauncey Gardner floating through the corridors of power. Not forgetting Inspector Jacques Clouseau, who always managed to land on his feet (when it wasn't somebody else's). So maybe our sense of loss derived from the fact that many people seemed to have died with Peter Sellers, not only those characters he'd already given unforgettable voice and face to but all the others he never had time to create. In a sense, there was quite a high death toll on that July day in 1980.

1 Going, Going... Goon!

PETER SELLERS wasn't born in a trunk, but he was brought up in one. His maternal grandmother, née Welcome but known professionally as Ma Ray, was a formidable lady by all accounts. With ten children in tow, including Peter's mother Peg, she launched what was to be England's first aquatics revue. It would tour the provincial music halls at the turn of the century, with – for the period – scantily dressed bathing beauties performing the sort of elementary feat whose only distinction was that it took place underwater. Eating a banana, for instance. It was in Huddersfield that the inevitable occurred: during a show entitled all too prophetically *Splash Me*, the huge German-manufactured tank burst, leaving, as they say, not a dry eye in the house.

Later the company was joined by a young piano-player named Bill Sellers, whose sole claim to fame (never substantiated) was that he had been British movie favorite George Formby's banjo teacher. In 1923, at the Bloomsbury Registrar's Office, he and Peg were married. Two years after that, on September 8, their son Peter was born in the coastal resort of Southsea. A plump little baby, he took after his mother who, Peter was subsequently to learn, took after *her* great grandfather, a celebrated barefisted prizefighter of confused Portuguese-Jewish origins, Daniel Mendoza. Though he died in poverty, Mendoza had once taught pugilism to George IV when still Prince of Wales. Peter was to become inordinately proud of this flamboyant ancestor.

Only weeks after his birth, the latest addition to Ma Ray's troupe, receiving a baptism of applause, was carried onto the stage by the show's comic. Peter responded in no less timeworn fashion, and his bawling brought the house down. Oddly enough this first scathing comment on the theater and its hallowed traditions proved lasting. Doubtless, sitting alone in sweaty dressing-rooms or fondled by overbearing baritones, Peter was already acquiring a taste for the roar of the crowd. But the smell of the greasepaint remained anathema to him all his life. According to Dennis Selinger, who became his first agent in 1946, Sellers did not hate the stage. "I think what Peter hated was not the theatre because he had a great admiration for a lot of theatrical actors – Olivier and Guinness were his idols – but the discipline of the theatre. In fact, I don't think – I know it. He could not or would not put himself in a position of having to do the same thing day in and day out for any length of time. He was too creative a person to knuckle down." The fact remains that Sellers, whose knack for disguise and dependence on vocal delivery for comic effect were eminently theatrical, only ever consented to star in one play, the farce *Brouhaha* in 1958.

Peg was both the archetypal Jewish mother and stage mother. She loved to spoil her only son, who was denied companions of his own age as the family flitted from town to town and dingy boarding-rooms to even dingier ones. She was desperately eager for him to follow in the footsteps of two generations. When it got obvious that Peter's ambitions ultimately lay elsewhere, coupled with the fact that Bill had formed a double act with a ukelele player, she reluctantly settled down in a house near Regent's Park in London. Though money was scarce, nothing less than a fee-paying private school, St. Mark's Kindergarten, was good enough for Peter.

Later they moved to Highgate, Peg opening a small antique shop and Peter switching to an exclusive Catholic college – this for the son of Jewish and Protestant parents! And in 1939, when Peter was 14, they moved again – to another resort, Ilfracombe in Devon, where one of Peg's many brothers ran the local variety show. Peter, who had succeeded in 'playing hookey' from the theater he detested so heartily, once more found himself within earshot of the roaring crowds. He laboriously made his way up from sweeping out after the performances through being ticket-collector, box-office, assistant stage manager front of house, lights, assistant stage manager, stage manager and finally, as he put it, "playing small parts like 'Your carriage is without' or 'Hello', minor tiddly-poo things".

With Bill on tour, Peter was completely under Peg's thumb. It's possible to speculate that, after her death, his fascination with clairvoyants – mostly feminine – represented a nebulous attempt to bolster his insecurity with some omniscient mother-figure. So long as his aspirations were rooted in show business, Peg faithfully encouraged them. For example, when she discovered that he was sneaking into the closed theater to improvise on drums left overnight in the orchestra pit, she

promptly purchased a set and paid for lessons. Though it's hard to believe
he would have been satisfied with the monotonous virtuosity of drum
solos *à la* Gene Krupa, Peter was ever after persuaded he could have
turned professional. But the diminutive theater in Ilfracombe also managed to draw some prestigious straight actors. After admiring Paul
Scofield as a psychopath in Emlyn Williams' hugely successful thriller
Night Must Fall, he startled his fellow performers with the sinister inflec-
tion he would give an innocuous line like 'Your carriage is without'. Even
his fleeting (and disastrous) endeavor to make a living as a private
detective in the Sam Spade vein probably derived more from his craving
to become an actor than from any genuine investigative abilities.

But, in the early '40s, there were rumblings off-stage in a more global
sense. With many eligible young musicians removed for military service,
vacancies in dance bands had become, so to speak, a Sellers market. Peter
soon found employment as stand-in drummer with both Oscar Rabin and

Henry Hall, bandleaders who were to broadcast frequently during the war. In 1943, however, now of enlistment age himself, he abandoned his current employers, an obscure combo named Waldini and his Gypsy Band, and joined the Royal Air Force. Thanks to vociferous protests from his mother, he was at first exempted from overseas duty. After spending a few desultory months as an armorer's assistant, he was co-opted into the RAF Gang Show, a wartime offshoot of Ralph Reader's Boy Scout Revues. As a chorus boy, he could hardly indulge his burgeoning taste for extravagant character roles. So, with a chum who was later to offer him support in 17 movies, David Lodge, Airman Second Class Sellers would infiltrate the Officers' Mess with his (suitably promoted) person. In these hoaxes undoubtedly originated the characterization of the feckless Flight Lieutenants of *Dr. Strangelove* and *Soft Beds, Hard Battles*. Once, with turban and boot-black, he even impersonated an officer of the Sikh Air Force, telling a few Sikh jokes in the curdled accent he later refined for the mild little Indian doctor of *The Millionairess*. Since he was never caught out, it's possible that only showbiz success dissuaded him from turning his mastery of disguises to more disreputable ends.

To describe being discharged from the army, the English employ a curious term: demob. Though 'mob' is in fact a contraction of 'mobilization', the word also suggests ceasing to be part of the mob. Recovering your identity. Yet, too often, the identity recovered after years of military service proved as ill-fitting as the regulation suit issued to every ex-serviceman. And like many of his badly tailored fellows, Peter realized that he had exchanged one mob for another: the mob of restless misfits scrabbling for the same few precious jobs. Suddenly London seemed to be teeming with drummers, all more talented and experienced than he. Accepting the gigs that were refused by the professionals, he began to wonder if there mightn't be an easier way to earn a living than toting a cumbersome set of drums out to some grim provincial dance hall. Since his happiest days in the Air Force had been spent in the uniform of a genial, moustachioed Air Marshall coolly and condescendingly hob-nobbing with the lower orders (who were actually his superiors), he decided to become a mimic.

Peg was delighted, and even Bill briefly surfaced to teach his son the rudiments of the ukelele. It was decided that the time had come to interest an agent. Which is where Dennis Selinger comes in, a man who, in spite of professional differences, was to remain Sellers' lifelong friend. In 1946 he too had just been demobbed and was employed by a small but respectable theatrical agency. "I had a visit from Peg, saying that she had a son who was very talented and a potential star. He was then what was called Entertainments Manager at Parkin's Holiday Camp in Jersey. So I went to see him compéring Sunday concerts and doing his stand-up act . . . and, well, I liked him." Almost at once they became close friends. "Possibly because we were more or less the same age and we had vaguely said hello in India when I was serving there and he came out with a Gang Show. It happens with agencies. You are drawn towards one person and it just builds from there.'' What did he see in Peter Sellers, Entertainments Manager? "Without any doubt at all, I saw a real talent. Timing. Star quality. At that stage, of course, I had no illusions of his ever breaking into films. The act I saw him do consisted of his telling virtually one, protracted story – about an Englishman, an Irishman and a Welshman, as I remember – and he would switch hats and accents with each nationality. He already possessed an incredible vocal facility.''

With Selinger behind him, Sellers began to be offered regular bookings all over the country. But his progress at this period of his career was horizontal, not vertical. Nothing yet suggested that he would rise to the top of any bill, however provincial, let alone soar off it into international stardom. At his lowest ebb, he auditioned for the Windmill Theatre in London's Soho. A strip joint run by impresario Vivian Van Damm whose motto 'We Never Closed' was jocularly lisped into 'We Never Clothed', it used a regular supply of stand-up comics to populate the stage while the girls changed their G-strings. Sellers duly completed a six-week stint, his comedy-cum-impersonation routine being greeted with the same intense and deafening silence as the strippers themselves, if doubtless for very different reasons. The comics who worked there could usually be divided into two categories: the hopeful and the hopeless. Oddly enough, though Sellers' own success was very much run-of-the-Windmill, Van Damm had sufficient savvy to have his name inscribed on a bronze plaque: Stars Of Today Who Started Their Careers In This Theatre, the day following the comic's unlamented departure instead of, as was the custom, a full year later. It was preceded by that of another young unknown whose future was to be linked with Sellers': Harry Secombe.

If it offered no irrefutable evidence of a unique potential, Sellers' experience at the Windmill proved at least that he possessed the kind of nerve required to walk fully clothed onto the stage – of a strip joint. This asset was very much to the fore when he again attempted to deploy his vocal abilities in furtherance of his career. Sellers decided to ring up Roy Speer, a producer of BBC Radio Light Entertainment, and ask for an audition. But as always, off-stage no less than on, he felt considerably more assured when enveloped in an alien identity; so that, when Speer's secretary came on the line, Sellers, mildly panic-stricken, almost automatically slipped into the plummy tones of one of the period's broadcasting luminaries, Kenneth Horne, After a ritual exchange of pleasantries, 'Horne' began to enthuse at length on a brilliantly original comedian whose act had recently played at the Windmill. He even persuaded his own partner in comedy, 'Richard Murdoch' (guess who?), to support him in his extravagant claims. Duly impressed by their recommendation, Speer agreed to interview the up-and-coming genius; and it was then that Sellers, having taken the bull by the Horne, as it were, reverted to his normal, somewhat colorless voice and timidly suggested that they meet as soon as possible. Following a moment's hesitation, when sheer fury at being so duped debated with a professional's grudging admiration for such faultless mimicry, Speer gracefully capitulated and ordered Sellers to come to his office at once.

This now legendary anecdote serves to demonstrate the degree to which, paradoxically, Sellers has never really been a 'character actor'. His multiple impersonations, his talent for peopling the space around him with a ghostly entourage proved to be a curiously direct reflection of some deep-seated sense of personal inferiority which, no matter how great his success, he never quite succeeded in eradicating. In a sense it was when he played someone else, preferably with an exotic accent, that he became most himself.

The telephone ruse worked. Like Selinger before him, Speer was shrewd enough to detect the presence of a true original behind Sellers' cheeky blandness, and he allotted him a five-minute slot on a radio variety show called, with breathtaking invention, *Show Time*. Other radio and music hall dates followed, and he even found himself top of the bill, albeit in a suburban theater – the Plaza, West Bromwich – that was fairly close to the bottom as a venue for vaudeville stars. But perhaps a greater boost to his (and his mother's) well-being was his very first press cutting, from the London *Evening News*. The article, entitled *This Mimic Is Tops*, read:

'O. Henry once spoke of an actor who "did impersonations of well-known impersonators". Certainly many mimics give too little study to their originals. Peter Cavanagh [before Sellers, the most famous of British mimics] is an exception.

'And now, in Peter Sellers, radio brings us another really conscientious and excellent artist and a genuine rival to Cav.

'Tall, goodlooking, 22, Sellers was born in Portsmouth of a theatrical family. Entertaining in the war days, he was carefully studying famous radio voices. His first broadcast in "Show Time" recently brought a scurry of agents and he's already fixed up a long series of Sunday concerts all over the country; and Roy Speer immediately booked him for the first available return date in "Show Time".'

Soon a more lasting bond, that of friendship, was to be forged between those two names so fortuitously linked on the Windmill plaque, Peter Sellers and Harry Secombe. Sellers met Secombe, a roly poly pudding of a Welshman and by universal accord 'the nicest man in the business', while the latter was appearing in a provincial show whose innocently intended title would be well nigh unthinkable today: *Soldiers in Skirts*. Later, backstage, he was introduced to Secombe's friends, Spike Milligan, a chronically unstable creature whose madness was rendered more than tolerable by the fact of being screamingly funny, and Michael Bentine, an Eton educated ex-Shakespearean actor with a Peruvian scientist father. In spite of such vast divergences of background, all four had one thing in common: a taste for off-beat (or rather – as one says 'off-off-Broadway' – off-off-beat) humor that managed to encompass the Anglo-Saxon nonsense tradition of Carroll, Lear, Leacock and even, in view of their penchant for outrageous wordplay, James Joyce; the Marx Brothers; and what might be called International Surrealism in drag. Milligan, one of whose favorite pranks consisted of knocking on an undertaker's door, crying out 'Shop!', then closing his eyes, folding his hands solemnly across his chest and lying down on the sidewalk, had at that time cramped lodgings in a pub owned by Jimmy Grafton, a scriptwriter who had returned from the war with a Military Cross earned at the Battle of Arnhem in 1944. That evening, therefore, the improbable quartet opted to continue their conversation at Grafton's, which would soon serve as their regular hangout.

Little by little, the ad lib quadruple act that they were almost unconsciously building up had been so perfected until it was virtually a series of brilliantly eccentric comedy sketches. One day Grafton proposed that they make a recording together and pass it on to an acquaintance of his at the BBC, producer Pat Dixon. After a few false starts, the program finally invaded the air waves as 'Crazy People, featuring Radio's own Crazy Gang – The Goons!' That was May 28, 1951.

Since the task of defining the humor of the Goons to a layman would require a volume to itself, it's fortunate that few people with even the vaguest interest in show business can claim never to have caught any of their shows, either when originally broadcast or in one of countless reruns. So rapid was the spread of their success that one may still encounter some total stranger from New Jersey or New South Wales and discover that one shares memories – of listening to the old Goon Shows on steam radio (a term that must have seemed faintly archaic even in the early '50s). Who, having once encountered them, can ever forget The Dreaded Batter Pudding Hurler, The Affair of the Lone Banana or The Tay Bridge Disaster, this last starring William McGoonagle, perpetrator of shaggy doggerel and a still more atrocious poet than the notorious Scottish versifier, McGonagle, on whom he was based?

For sheer anarchistic invention, radio was the rival of both the printed word and cartoonery. Print because, as in a novel but unlike the theater or, to a lesser extent, cinema and television, anything was possible. A cast of thousands could be persuasively conjured up with just a single recording from the archives; the listener could be transported to the other side of the globe and back again (one always had the sneaking suspicion that an announcer, claiming to be speaking from, say, Calcutta was actually installed in a neighboring studio); and a producer, with no more than a handful of sound effects, could center his show around some spectacular natural catastrophe. As in a cartoon, moreover, a multiplicity of characters might exist through one dimension only: in animation through line,

on radio through voice. And most attempts to translate these characteristics into a more intrinsically realistic medium – e.g. the Charlie Brown cartoon movies, the visualization of The Goons' 'sound slapstick' on TV's *A Show Called Fred* and *Son of Fred* – were doomed, at best, to crude approximation.

The Goon Show made unparalleled use of an extensive range of specifically radiophonic devices, its bizarre but oddly evocative noises-off hardly differing from the semi-articulate utterances by which the leading characters made themselves instantly recognizable and enduringly beloved. Eccles' ''Hellow dere'', Bluebottle's ''Ye he-he! Heuheuheuheuheu he!'' and Henry Crun's ''Mnk – grnk – mnk – mnk –grmp'' were all *reductio ad absurdum* parodies of a classic radio convention: the catch-phrase. The show was never less than generous in its 'locations', as when in one episode an English prison took its annual summer holiday on Devil's Island, or when the archcriminal Hercules Gritpype-Thynne was tracked down to Africa (''Africa, eh? We've got him cornered!''). It also helped that the three main performers (Bentine, whose personality was too closely related to Milligan's, gradually effaced himself) could, in cases of illness or indisposition, play each other's roles

Making the headlines i▸
first TV show, *Idiot's W*

without the listener ever being aware of the substitution. But Sellers above all was in his element and his gallery of 'funny voices' soon became an obsession among English adolescents, a malady from which the country as a whole has not yet recovered. I can still recall my own gratification as a teenager at having 'cracked' the pickled military intonations he earmarked for Major Bloodnok who, when greeted by an innocuous 'Hello', would bluster "How dare you accuse me of robbing the regimental cashbox!" Instead of skateboards, *the* craze in my youth was for Goonish patois: Neddy Seagoon's staccato "What-What-What?", Gritpype-Thynne's effetely nasal "You naughty man, you!" or, quite simply, any use of the word 'Fred' – a name that to the English is funny in itself. The rare photographs of Sellers made public at this period, with his impishly glinting glasses and crescent moon smile, also suggested a tiny tot decadence that was particularly appealing to us would-be precocious schoolboys.

The Goon Show ran, off and on, until January 1960. Apart from the *Fred* shows mentioned above, television called on the trio's talents for notably *The Idiot Weekly Price 2d, Yes, It's the Cathode Ray Tube Show* and a puppet series *The Telegoons*, none of which, despite incidental felicities, ever managed to catch the high-powered delirium of the original. But by the time, in April 1972, a valedictory edition *The Last Goon Show of All* was broadcast, it had become clear that, for better or worse, the Goons were now part of the national consciousness. The adjective 'Goonish' entered the language and, subsequently, the dictionary. The extraordinary verbal inventions of Milligan, especially when given flesh – in sound – by Sellers, altered our perception of that amorphous concept 'British humor', formerly the province of Ealing Films and their undoubted knack for depicting England as foreigners fondly but wishfully imagine it to be.

While the show's influence on *Monty Python*, for example, hardly needs to be underlined, its wider significance is more difficult to measure. The profound upheaval in public hierarchies and private morals that rocked ('n' rolled) England in the '60s was, of course, generated principally through a revolution in musical taste as personified by the Beatles. But the humor that was never absent from the movement came straight from the Goons. The director of the Beatles movies, Richard Lester, had launched his career in 1959 with an eleven-minute short, *The Running, Jumping and Standing Still Film*, which Sellers himself produced and starred in with Milligan, the two of them cavorting lunatically in a field. Oddly enough, similar pastoral capers punctuate both *A Hard Day's Night* and *Help!*; and the latter's complicated plotline, involving an ineptly ruthless Indian sect intent on recovering a sacred ring innocently purchased by Ringo at a Bond Street jewellers, might have been squeezed into a half-hour Goon Show. The Beatles' full-length cartoon *The Yellow Submarine*, their LP recording *Sergeant Pepper's Lonely Hearts Club Band* and the various odd jottings of John Lennon, *In His Own Write* and *A Spaniard in the Works*, all testified to Goonish inspiration.

Inspiration that was not only confined to England. Lester's Hollywood oeuvre (e.g. his farcical adaptation of *The Three Musketeers*) is shot through with a vein of 'British rubbish' that has never been indigenous to the classic screwball tradition of American comedy. (Although it was unfortunate that he and Sellers never collaborated on a feature, his antiwar satire *How I Won the War* and excellent movie version of John Antrobus' play about a post-nuclear England *The Bed Sitting Room* constituted perhaps the most faithful translations of Goon humor into another, *a priori* hostile medium.) Without Sellers' own international success, that of the Beatles and, later, the Monty Python team, it is

Springing a leek for St. David's Day (1956).

doubtful whether such director-comics as Mel Brooks (*Blazing Saddles*, *Young Frankenstein*), Gene Wilder (*Sherlock Holmes' Smarter Brother*, *The World's Greatest Lover*), Marty Feldman (*The Last Remake of Beau Geste*) and possibly even Woody Allen (*Bananas, Everything You Always Wanted To Know About Sex*) would have shaken up Hollywood's comedic conventions in quite the same manner.

To his credit, superstar Sellers never forgot the origins of his fame and prosperity. In his very last movie, the disappointing and uneven *The Fiendish Plot of Dr. Fu Manchu* (1980, directed by Piers Haggard and, allegedly, Sellers himself), one of the more peripheral characters was dubbed Warrington Minge, a name dripping with nostalgia for aficionados of the Goons. He was fond of surrounding himself, in supporting roles, with old friends from Grafton's pub, such as Graham Stark and David Lodge. And, none too happily ensconced in the expatriate colony of Beverly Hills or the vapid luxury of a Swiss lakeside villa, his warmest memories, to which he would obsessively return, were of the camaraderie of the BBC days. If ever he were depressed (a not infrequent

ellers or Gilbert
g the radio
ntator?

occurrence at the end of his life), he would pick up the telephone and reminisce across the Atlantic with Milligan or Secombe. Radio, akin to the telephone in the way it enables shy people to hold forth, was an ideal vehicle for his weird brand of extroversion by proxy; and later, when rebeling against the cinema's more stringent discipline, he would be assailed by nostalgia for the halcyon period when just three men around a single bulky microphone could conjure up a Surrealistic universe.

With the growing enthusiasm, both 'cult' and popular, for the Goons, Sellers' offstage character was beginning to receive media coverage. Though at this juncture of his life he could ill afford such indulgences, he had already bought no fewer than four automobiles, a passion for which he retained until his death. His wilful indiscipline, a positive asset on the *Goon Show*, had begun to antagonize a few theatrical impresarios; as once, to protest the icy reception that Milligan's act had met with in a Coventry music hall, he appeared on stage in an indecently scanty loincloth and created a one-man *tableau vivant* to the accompaniment of mellow big band recordings (and the bewildered dismay of the audience). And he had already established a reputation among his fellow comedians as a Romeo with a veritable harem of Juliets.

In 1949, however, at a charity ball organized by the vaudeville fraternity, the Grand Order of Water Rats, he encountered the real thing. Ironically, there *was* a vaguely star-crossed aspect to the affair in that the young woman he met and fell in love with – Anne Hayes, an Australian starlet who had played a small part in Korda's *Anna Karenina* with Vivien Leigh – had been escorted to the gala by Sellers' manager, Dennis Selinger. As Sellers began to spend more and more time in Anne's company, he became melodramatically persuaded that he had stolen his best friend's girl. For three long months, he never once dared to broach the subject. Selinger, on the other hand, was delighted with the romance of his protégés, the more so as he realized that what he had observed at the Water Rats' Ball (how that word 'rat' must have preyed on Sellers' mind!) was an authentic case of love at first sight.

The trouble with love at first sight, of course, is that it so rarely lasts to the second. But Peter and Anne were married eighteen months later – the longest 'engagement' he had enjoyed up to that time – on September 15 1951 at London's Caxton Hall. And they remained married for eleven years – which also proved by far the longest of Sellers' marriages. Anne was a pertly pretty blonde, very much her husband's 'type', who possessed a huge sense of humor coupled with a level-headedness that would both restrain and complement his moodiness as it increasingly verged on manic depression. Even Peg, who had resented another feminine presence in Peter's life before he had really made the grade, was compelled to admit that Anne's strength of character could only have a beneficial effect on her son's volatile personality.

So Peter was married. He appeared to be settling down. He was widely recognized as a uniquely gifted radio performer. Only one peak remained to be scaled, but it was the Everest of every young hopeful's ambition in show business: the movies.

P.S. with his first wif
(Howe) in 1951.

2 In A Sellers' Market

SELLERS when interviewed for *Films and Filming*, March 1960:
"Doing *The Goon Show* series had some drawbacks. As far as filmmaking
is concerned and as far as one's part in films as a character actor is
concerned, many filmmakers tend to think of you as a funny voice man
instead of being a serious actor." In fact, not a few of his initial 'appearances' in movies were for voice only. He dubbed everybody and everything from Bogart in John Huston's camp thriller parody *Beat the Devil*
(when the star was unavailable for post-synchronization) to Churchill's
voice in the espionage movie *The Man Who Never Was* (directed by
Ronald Neame) and even a parrot in an extended desert island joke, *Our
Girl Friday*, featuring Joan Collins in the title role. In *Malaga* (aka *Fire
Over Africa*) he is said to have dubbed several performers – of both sexes!
All of which must have contributed to his uneasy impression of becoming 'the man who never was' around the British studios. When he did
appear in person, as in *London Entertains* (1951), it was as . . . himself.
This showbiz travelog consisted of a tour conducted by radio and later TV
personality Eamonn Andrews through Battersea Festival, the Windmill
Theatre, a West End nightclub and a BBC studio where the Goons were in
rehearsal.

A real part was finally offered him as a querulous Major in a minor
comedy, *Penny Points to Paradise* (1951, directed by Tony Young), about
a football pools winner (Sellers' old chum Harry Secombe) who spends a
holiday at a Brighton boarding house where he attracts the attention of a
pretty young fortune hunter and an unscrupulous pair of counterfeiters.

It boasted a musical interlude with a long forgotten but unforgettably named orchestra: Felix Mendelssohn and his Hawaiian Serenaders! Three years later, while he was starring in the pantomime 'Mother Goose' at the London Palladium, he filmed *Orders Are Orders*, a farce centered around the invasion of a British regimental depot by a Hollywood film unit. So loosely was it based on the original play (by Ian Hay and Anthony Armstrong) that it risked becoming wholly detached from it; but it was a useful showcase for the as yet untapped talents of two major English comedians, Sellers in the role of a lowly Private and the much-regretted Tony Hancock.

Sellers, as he himself was doubtless aware, was poised on the very brink of the Big Time. This is a particularly affecting, exhilarating moment in any performer's career, for in show business it's paradoxically on the first rung of the ladder that one feels most dizzy and light-headed. For Sellers the turning point came, after another supporting performance as a policeman in *John and Julie* (1955, directed by William Fairchild), in the form of a blessing in disguise. Selinger had heard that the Ealing director Alexander Mackendrick (*The Man in the White Suit*, *The Maggie*) was beginning to cast his latest comedy, *The Ladykillers*. Sellers was rejected in the thuggish part he auditioned for, and which was played in the movie by Danny Green, but so impressed MacKendrick that he was offered a smaller — but in the event more memorable — role as a pudgy, incompetent Teddy Boy henchman. And it was *The Ladykillers*, an enormous commercial and critical success in both the UK and USA, that definitively turned him into a movie actor.

There was an oddly satisfying rightness about his launching a new career in one of the last of the Ealing comedies, given that it was his experience with the Goons that was ushering in a whole new concept in British humor. No less appropriate was the fact that he should be playing opposite one of his idols, the multi-faceted actor who had personified Ealing's more genteel tradition of farce and who had formerly cornered the market in vocal versatility and virtuosity: Alec Guinness (here, as the toothily macabre Professor, apparently imitating Alastair Sim). Not that *The Ladykillers* was conspicuously genteel; on the contrary, it proved to be one of the most cruelly hilarious films ever produced by the studio. William Rose's ingenious screenplay concerned dear old Mrs. Wilberforce (a *tour de force* of affectionately observed dottiness from the veteran character actress Katie Johnson), on whom it gradually dawns that the Professor and his four dubious accomplices who meet in her tiny house, a country cottage incongruously located near King's Cross Station in the heart of the metropolis (in itself an apt symbol for the Ealing style), are not the string quintet she had naively supposed them to be but a ruthless gang of thieves whose booty has been stuffed inside their instrument cases. Murdering her, however, as they fully intend to do, proves strangely impossible; it is they who are eliminated one by one by their blithely

The last film before the 'breakthrough.' P.S. pla local bobby – *John and J* (1955).

unruffled landlady, until at last the Professor himself receives a fatal karate chop from a railway signal post and tumbles headlong into a passing goods wagon.

As much as from the basic situation, the movie's black humor, (counterpointed by deceptively cheerful British Technicolor whose overall tonality seems determined by the primary childlike red of London's buses) derives from the precisely delineated identities of the five criminals and their intended victim. As Penelope Houston remarked in the Monthly Film Bulletin, they become "characters substantial enough for one to feel a certain inappropriate regret at their violent ends". Apart from Guinness's bungling evil genius and Sellers' whining milquetoast of a Teddy Boy, there is Cecil Parker's seedy Major, gathering about his person the shreds of a former respectability, Danny Green's monosyllabic bully boy and Herbert Lom's trigger-happy professional killer. And perhaps the moment when Sellers first demonstrated on screen the uner-

ring accuracy of his powers of *facial* expression was the scene in which
they are all being upbraided by Mrs. Wilberforce and, as she momentarily
turns away, a cello case concealed on the roof (for reasons too complicated to explain here) slides down into Sellers' arms. His embarrassed
dismay when Katie Johnson suddenly confronts him with it is a brilliant
cameo that brings a fundamentally 'unfocused' emotion into excrutiat-
ingly sharp focus. Along with Guinness and Katie Johnson's belated
'comeback', it was he who received most of the critics' attention.

One thing had been made clear: Peter Sellers was not just a funny voice.
He was an *actor*. Though enthusiasm for the Goons continued unabated,
attempts being made at this period to branch out into television, he
instinctively adopted a much more realistic tone for the movie screen –
indulging a penchant for an almost Chaplinesque 'Little Man' persona
that had been totally absent from his radio work. In this he differed from
his two collaborators. Neither for the natural born clownery of Secombe

(as Sellers commented, "Harry is just a funny person: he looks funny, he says funny things, he wakes up funny and goes to bed funny at night") nor for the unclassifiable lunacy of Milligan could a place be found in cinema, as was proved by a couple of inconclusive ventures. Not that Sellers' triumphs ever impaired their friendship: according to Jimmy Grafton, "There was absolutely no professional jealousy – to the end. They all laughed too much in each other's company for that to happen." (It *is* true that, after Sellers' death, Milligan was guest on a TV chat show and with typical unpredictability hinted at a more jaundiced view of their relationship.)

Sellers' next role, in Basil Dearden's gentle comedy *The Smallest Show on Earth* (1957), was as Leslie Quill, a cinema projectionist as old, flyblown and decrepit as the movie theater in which he worked. He was co-starred opposite two stalwart originals of British stage and screen, Bernard Miles, now Director of the Mermaid Theatre in London's dockland, and Margaret Rutherford, a cosy Cheshire Cat of an actress who left grins on other people's faces. Together, they managed – in the nicest possible way – to steal the film from its nominal leads, Bill Travers and Virginia McKenna (who were later to find nursing Elsa the Lioness in *Born Free* a more congenial proposition).

In the same year he starred in Mario Zampi's *The Naked Truth*. A pleasant, vulgar but undeniably funny film about the victims of a smooth blackmailer conspiring to liquidate him, it was important for Sellers as his first encounter with the multiple role playing essayed with such elegance by Guinness in *Kind Hearts and Coronets*. In fact, he played only one role, but his Wee Sonny McGregor – a much-loved television personality harboring a dark secret in his closet – was, like Sellers himself, a master of mimicry, which gave the actor an opportunity to impersonate a plodding policeman, a Cockney bargee and an old white-haired Chelsea Pensioner. The most amusing moment involved this last disguise. A fact unknown to his legion of fans, Wee Sonny is also a wealthy landlord, extorting outrageous rents for his rat-infested slum dwellings from a number of unfortunate senior citizens (which is, of course, why he has become the object of blackmail). To his horror, one of the guests on his TV show, a medal-beribboned Pensioner begins to fulminate against McGregor's apartments of which he is a dissatisfied tenant. Sonny's attempts to silence him – at first with studied casualness, then with increasingly staccato inflections and helplessly flailing arm – perfectly convey the horror of coping with a gaffe on live television.

Professionally, 1958 was a crowded year for him, each of his three movies enhancing his reputation and revealing unsuspected sides to his talent. (It was about this time that Bob Hope, in England to make a movie, cracked, "It's an experimental film. It doesn't star Peter Sellers.") In *Up the Creek* a routine naval farce with David Tomlinson and Wilfred Hyde White, his characterization of an Irish Petty Officer was so much more

three-dimensional than the stock 'types' with which it was surrounded
that it tended to unbalance the film. Sellers, obviously, was too subtle an
observer of human frailties to be entirely comfortable in traditional British comedy. *tom thumb* (directed by George Pal), though mostly shot in
England, was his first Hollywood financed movie. An enchanting fantasy
for children 'of all ages' with splendidly inventive special effects and
dancer Russ Tamblyn (or should one say 'russ tamblyn'?) in the diminutive title role, it featured Sellers and Terry-Thomas as the villains (hiss!)
and demonstrated that he could extend his range to accommodate pure
knockabout slapstick. Here his antics with the suave, gap-toothed

29

Confrontation on board
between "Cooky" (John
Warren) and "Bosun" –
Up the Creek (1958).

Thomas approached the comic anarchy of such cartoon duos as Tom and Jerry or Sylvester and Tweety Pie. He then agreed to make a guest appearance in another Pal fairy tale, *The Wonderful World of the Brothers Grimm*, but eventually backed out: which was just as well, as that indigestible Cinerama epic proved more Grimm than wonderful.

In his third film of the year, *Carlton-Browne of the F.O.* (F.O. standing for 'Foreign Office'), a comedy of international diplomacy starring Terry-Thomas once more, Ian Bannen and Luciana Paoluzzi, he played Amphibulous, a smooth Levantine politician complete with crumpled white suit, oily black forelock and moustache from beneath which protruded an eternally moist cheroot. Sellers strolled through the part which offered him few opportunities, except for five minutes of drollery when, at an official airport reception, he and the newly arrived Governor-General solemnly march past each other on a smoke-filled tarmac. But the movie was useful in that it effected a meeting between him and the Boulting Brothers, the terrible twins of British comedy, whose productions, after the unexpected box-office success in New York of *Private's Progress*, were all but guaranteed American distribution.

His next, *The Mouse That Roared* (directed by Jack Arnold), which might be described as an international Ealing comedy, turned out to be one of 1959's 'sleepers': as Sellers himself, who did not care for it overmuch, remarked in an interview, "In the first four weeks of its American run it took over a million dollars, which is more money than any other British picture ever to play there has taken in the same length of time. In New York they were queueing four deep, if you please, from the Guild Cinema right round the block." An extremely minor and only mildly amusing satire, *The Mouse That Roared* is worth taking a closer look at as it represented the summation of Sellers' past achievements and foreshadowed the kind of transatlantic career that lay ahead.

Its plot (from the novel by Leonard Wibberly) revolved around the decision of a tiny bankrupt state in Central Europe, the Duchy of Grand Fenwick, to declare war on the USA in the ostensibly justifiable hope of losing almost immediately, so reaping the traditional benefits of such a defeat: aid given, money lent, roads, harbors and hospitals built. But, as is the way with these schemes (think of Zero Mostel's plan to stage a theatrical flop with 'Springtime for Hitler' in Mel Brooks' *The Producers*), Grand Fenwick is *victorious* – by accidentally capturing an atomic scientist along with his latest, most lethal bomb. The Ealing reference is evident – especially when 'Fenwick', as the name of a Central European country, is seen as the reverse of London's Italianate 'Pimlico' in *Passport to Pimlico*. No less evident is the influence of *The Goon Show*, in the topsy-turvy situation and much of the off-beat humor: the Grand Fenwickian government sends its official Declaration of Hostilities through the mail, at the frontier post is erected a sign 'If guard not on duty, go right in', etc.

The Mouse that Roared (1959). "Count Mount prepares for war with the USA...

... whilst "Grand Duchess Gloriana" plays on ...

In this, his first starring role, Sellers actually did play three separate characters (plus being briefly glimpsed as the statue of Sir Roger Fenwick, the Duchy's founder). Most effective was the Duchess herself, playing the harpsichord or graciously taking leave of a representative from the State Department with "Give my love to your President — and Mrs. Coolidge, too". There was also the Prime Minister, whose elegant goatee, monocle and George Sanderish tones brought Gritpype-Thynne to the screen. Together, the Duchess and her PM (whom she affectionately nicknames 'Bobo', the title of a future Sellers comedy) suggested a homage both to the Alec Guinness of *Kind Hearts and Coronets* and his Disraeli opposite Irene Dunne's Queen Victoria in *The Mudlark*. But Sellers' third characterization, the unprepossessing Tully Bascombe, reluctant Commander-in-Chief of the handful of soldiers in Grand Fenwick's army, made a disappointingly flat and colorless impression — precisely because it wasn't an *impression*. As he was to prove at the end of his life in *Being There*, he could lend vivid existence to a character absolutely devoid of psychological substance, but he never learned how to play 'himself'. With no more than his own pair of glasses as comic props, causing him in his Fenwickian coat of armor to resemble a

plumper Woody Allen, he was visibly at a loss to breathe life into Tully or make the romance between him and the scientist's daughter (Jean Seberg) anything but tedious and unconvincing. It was a mistake which he was rarely to repeat.

The detested smell of greasepaint and failure had given way to the sweeter one of success. Peter Sellers had proved to the world and himself that he was an actor: now had come the longed for moment of stardom. And he was determined to live like a star. He moved out of a comfortable family home in the lush commuter belt of Whetstone, just at the frontier of London and the greenery of Hertfordshire, into a costly Tudor manor house at Chipperfield, where that same county borders the even lusher Buckinghamshire. He acquired the *sine qua non* of cinema folk: a swimming pool. Plus five acres of garden. Plus stables. Plus a butler. A groom. A nanny. A gardener. An ever-expanding menagerie of exotic birds and beasts. And a vast model railway circuit. And even, for the movie star who has everything, a mechanical elephant! Seeing himself now as a country squire, he immediately began to dress and speak the part, as if for a movie role, dropping into his local pub in tweedy suits and deerstalker hat. And one after the other, a fleet of sleek automobiles would race through his life as rapidly as on a speedway track.

But, according to those friends and journalists who visited him at this period, Sellers was not a happy man. Though now the parents of two children, Michael and Sarah, relations between Anne and himself were increasingly strained. He had never pretended to be the easiest person in the world to live with, but his chronic moodiness had now become perceptible to even casual acquaintances. It's possible that for actors, just as for the moviegoing public in general, the cinema represents a form of psychological escapism. Sellers, unsatisfied with his long-running 'role' as husband and father, would seek consolation for his boredom by clambering inside another character's skin and plunging – voice-first, as it were – into an artificial arc-lit world, like a diver in an all-enveloping rubber suit. He was accepted as a ruthless perfectionist, with all that the designation implies in irritability toward those around him (including Anne). "I hate everything I do so much," he was reported to have said, "that I always think I'm going to go one better before I die. I mean, I always think there's something left in me. I know there is – there's something in here somewhere that I want to get out." To which might be added a chilling phrase from another interview: "The character starts to get into me, to take over, as in a trance. . . ."

Sellers was also beginning to acquire another reputation, one that is dreaded in every agent's office: that of 'temperamental'. The need to immerse himself in alien identities did not, it seems, preclude a monstrous ego. In the early months of 1958, he appeared on the legitimate stage (for the first and last time) in a farce set in an Arab sheikdom, *Brouhaha* by George Tabori. The play had a successful run at the Aldwych Theatre, now the home of the Royal Shakespeare Company. But Sellers made himself notorious for his lack of discipline and, in particular, his unethical tendency to ad lib, a habit that is calculated to amuse an audience (whose applause for an actor fluffing his lines is often more indulgent than when he utters them with perfect lucidity) but can be a nightmare for fellow performers. On one memorable occasion, Sellers was suffering a king-sized hangover from the previous evening's revelry, a spectacularly merry party which Alec Guinness had given to celebrate his knighthood. The following day, to sustain him through a hard shooting schedule, he had taken enough hairs from the dog that bit him to fit out one of the false moustaches he was so fond of sporting. When, at eight o'clock that evening, he walked unsteadily onto the Aldwych stage, he was more than a little under the influence – and not of Guinness (either the actor or the drink)! After a few minutes floundering helplessly around the dramatist's lines, he stepped forward to the footlights and, for once, addressed the audience in his own voice: "I'm sloshed." But, unlike in the bad old days, the public made it vociferously clear that it was Peter Sellers, drunk or sober, whom they'd come to see, not his understudy, and he stumbled through what remained of the play (and at one point

"...ite" reads the riot act ...anagement after the ...as been unearthed – *Right, Jack* (1959).

stumbled off the stage into the orchestra pit) to receive a standing ovation at curtain call. Such enthusiasm for taboo theatrical behavior was not shared by the management.

In late 1958, Sellers was approached by the Boulting Brothers for a role in their next movie, a sequel to *Private's Progress* entitled *I'm All Right, Jack* (the title of the original novel by Alan Hackney, *Private Life*, was felt to bear too close a resemblance to that of Noël Coward's play, *Private Lives*). The script called for an obstinate, bloody-minded but well meaning trade union representative, Fred Kite, who, though not the film's leading character, was by far the most amusing and accurately observed. (The other protagonists, all held over from the earlier film, were to be played by Ian Carmichael, Terry-Thomas and Richard Attenborough.) To John Boulting's fury, Sellers turned the part down. Repeatedly. He reasoned that at this precarious stage of his career he really needed a starring role, which Kite wasn't, and even a sympathetic, almost romantic role, which Kite emphatically wasn't. He was also disappointed that Kite seemed to have been given relatively few 'funny lines', a startling remark in view of the way he subsequently took over the film but forgivable when one considers that he was accustomed to measuring a role's comic potential exclusively in terms of the number of gags clearly outlined in the script. He didn't fully understand that *I'm All Right, Jack*, a comedy of character and situation, was never intended to provoke guffaws.

With all the considerable charm he could muster, Boulting laid siege to Sellers, and his powers of persuasion were eventually effective: the actor

No way through for 'Br
Carmichael.

agreed to make a test. As always when preparing a new part, the first
hurdle to be overcome was the voice, which he arrived at through the
painstaking study of newsreel footage featuring prominent figures from
the trade union movement. Then came a Spartan, close-cropped, short-
back-and-sides haircut. And finally an ill-fitting double-breasted suit
carefully selected from the stock at Berman's, the trade's leading cos-
tumier. When Sellers walked onto the set and eerily began to spout Fred
Kite's platitudes, Boulting and his crew were temporarily silenced: more
than ever before, the actor had succeeded totally in submerging himself
in the character he was playing. Sellers, formerly a Jack of all parts, had
suddenly become the Master of one.

The brief prologue to *I'm All Right, Jack* is set in a sedately elegant
London club, from one of whose deep leather armchairs a white-haired
old gentleman (played, naturally, by Sellers himself) rises and, with
creaking steps, walks out of the room. On the soundtrack we hear a
narrator's voice intoning: "Take a last look at Sir John — he's on his way
out." Abruptly, the parodic rock 'n' roll theme tune explodes over the
credit titles and the movie is off. Its indiscriminate shafts of satire, aimed

both at what the filmmakers saw as the congenital laziness of the British worker (the factory strike around which the plotline is structured has been triggered off by someone working *too hard*) and the no less congenital chicanery of the British capitalist, also encompassed such related targets as time-and-motion experts, union bullying and automation. Though much of it must now appear dated and facile (there is a running gag involving a stutter which invariably besets its sufferer as he struggles with adjectives beginning with the letter 'f'), it surfaced at a period when the working class had been virtually unrepresented on screen and was greeted by both critics and public as a bracing antidote to the conventional crime comedies currently popular. It cocked a snook (or rather, made the offensive V-sign) at a whole herd of sacred cows, paving the way for the more subtle Cambridge-based satire of the *Beyond the Fringe* team and television's *That Was The Week That Was* in the '60s.

But its ultimate reputation undoubtedly depended on Sellers' performance. Whether perched on a soapbox, blowing his whistle and shouting "Everybody out!" or wistfully daydreaming about the joys of life in the Soviet Union "All them cornfields and ballet in the evening . . .", Kite instantly made a niche for himself in the collective English conscious-

37

ness. Though the Boultings portrayed him as a figure of comedy, Sellers prevented him for ever becoming a figure of fun. Apart from Ian Carmichael's chinless Candide of a hero (who takes refuge at the end in a nudist colony with his father, played by that splendidly double-chinless old character actor, Miles Malleson), Kite was oddly enough the movie's only sympathetic character: a well-intentioned man who patently cared about the welfare of his fellow workers, even if his rabid adherence to union tactics run rampant could only lead to disaster. And again, Sellers offered a technically brilliant cameo of extreme discomfort in the scene where Kite has been invited to discuss the implications of the strike on a TV news program. Beside him on the panel, another guest (the disillusioned Carmichael) is noisily fidgeting with the carafe of water which has been placed before him. Kite's distraction, as he valiantly attempts to set forth the workers' grievances, was caught by Sellers with preternatural vividness, that cloudiest of emotional states – public embarrassment – being decomposed into a series of gestural spasms which render his predicament almost painful to watch. *I'm All Right, Jack* was the finest opportunity ever presented to Sellers by the British cinema, which rewarded his performance with an Academy Award.

He followed it with a much less demanding role, that of the mild little Scottish accountant, Mr. Martin, in *The Battle of the Sexes*, an agreeably lightweight Ealing comedy directed by Charles Crichton and based on James Thurber's short story *The Catbird Seat*. When Martin's position of authority in a long-established Edinburgh textile firm is suddenly threatened by the arrival of Mrs. Barrow (Constance Cummings), an American efficiency expert who has charmed his boss (Robert Morley) into allowing her to shake up the firm's tried, tested but traditionalist methods, he is obliged to resort to desperate and very uncharacteristic measures. With his drooping moustache, his neat black brolly and his flawless imitation of the soft-spoken accent of old-world Edinburgh (far removed from any trace of cod Harry Lauder), Sellers beautifully judged the rising panic of a timid man, caught like a stag, at bay. The highlight of the film – and one of his most effective essays in purely physical comedy – was his attempt to seduce, then murder the formidable Mrs. Barrow. A crescendo of mishaps is crowned by the moment when Martin, having concealed the murder instrument – a kitchen knife – inside a drawer, fumbles behind his back to retrieve it while his intended victim unsuspectingly prepares cocktails for two. He finds it, raises it high over her shoulder-blades – only to discover to his horror that what he is brandishing is an egg-beater!

It was at this period that Sellers, another of whose idols was the great French performer-director Jacques Tati, had become obsessed with the arguable notion that comedy, to be truly international, should dispense with dialogue altogether. To prove his point, he produced *The Running, Jumping and Standing Still Film*. When it won first prize (the Golden

Gate Award) for the best short film at the San Francisco Festival, he remarked in an interview: "I've managed to get British Lion interested in this kind of film, and we may do a series of short abstract comedies. I would like to make a full-length one, not necessarily abstract comedy but a silent film in that respect, with some music and sound effects." Though what he was describing did indeed make for a hugely money-spinning comedy almost two decades later, Mel Brooks's *Silent Movie*, mimicry, not mime, was Sellers' forte; and there was surely something suicidally perverse in this urge to deny the very mainspring of his genius. But, as we will see, in his collaboration with director Blake Edwards on the *Pink Panther* cycle and especially *The Party*, Tati's influence, however coarsened, remained perceptible.

His last film of 1960, *Two Way Stretch* (directed by Robert Day), was an amiable prison farce which, though droll enough in its derivative fashion, can hardly be said to have stretched the talent of its leading performer. And it was doubtless his apprehension that he had as yet failed to capitalize on the triumph of *I'm All Right, Jack*, his sense of having allowed his career merely to coast along since that breakthrough, that led him to accept the role of Lionel Meadows, a sadistic gangster in a violent X-rated drama, *Never Let Go* (directed by John Guillermin). To be sure, compared with his co-stars – the insipid Richard Todd, whose upper lip appeared to have permanently stiffened after a glut of war movies, and pop singer Adam Faith, playing the kind of 'crazy mixed-up kid' typical of that coffee-bar era – Sellers gave a watchable and intermittently compelling performance in a register that was alien to him. But it was disappointing that for his first venture into dramatic cinema (a logical move for him to make in view of the depth he had lent to Kite) he had not chosen a worthier vehicle than this turgid thriller. And its feeble commercial (and critical) returns may explain why, with one exception he never again dared to relinquish the reassuring envelope of comedy.

The role caused ripples in his private life, however, with a marriage that was now heading for the rocks. Sellers had never found it easy to 'snap out' of a character's tics once the day's shooting had ended, a not too disturbing tendency as long as the role was that of a shy little clerk or a saintly Indian doctor. But he seemed no more capable of 'letting go' of Lionel Meadows, on occasion startling Anne and frightening the children with his displays of boorishness. As Dennis Selinger remarked: "Both film and role were a dreadful mistake, but Peter felt too tempted by the opportunity of extending his range to turn them down. He was, however, particularly prickly during that whole period."

Extending himself: this was his *idée fixe*. As is usually the case, ambition rewarded only leads to further ambition. In the decade since he had made his cinema début in *Penny Points to Paradise*, Sellers had completed no fewer than fourteen features, an impressive record. He had undoubtedly become the most popular and admired of British come-

dians. And he was about to be voted film actor of the year (for *The Mouse That Roared*, *Two Way Stretch*, *Never Let Go* and *The Millionairess*) by the Variety Club of Great Britain. What more could he wish for? Well, frustrated with being a big fish in a relatively little pond, he wanted to be the biggest fish of all in the ocean – and, in the cinema's terms, that ocean could only be Hollywood. What other fringe benefits are made available to movie superstars? Affairs with their leading ladies? Directing their own films? Making their first million? All of these enviable achievements would be his before the following decade ended. And yet. . . .

The ruthless "Lionel Meadows" exerts press the hapless "John Cummings" (Richard T – *Never Let Go* (1961).

3 From Millionairess To Millionaire

GEORGE BERNARD SHAW'S *Pygmalion* constitutes almost a unique case in the theater, that of a masterpiece (minor, perhaps, but authentic) which subsequently inspired another masterpiece, the musical *My Fair Lady*. With its example in mind, one cannot help regretting that another of his plays (and no masterpiece), *The Millionairess*, did not undergo the same transformation. A charming if rather woolly satire centered on Epifania, the richest woman in the world, all of whose wealth is insufficient to purchase the affection or respect of an impoverished Egyptian doctor who has devoted his life to ministering to the poor in London's East End, it would have made a delightful operetta. In the event, what one tends to remember most fondly from the film version (directed by Anthony Asquith from an adaptation by Wolf Mankowitz) is not on the screen at all: the sprightly duet "Goodness Gracious Me!" sung by Sellers and his co-star Sophia Loren on a record issued concurrently with the film's release.

Unfortunately, in *The Millionairess* itself, Asquith and his screenwriter effected a kind of Pygmalion metamorphosis in reverse, transforming a witty conversation piece into a stilted, studio-bound romantic comedy, in which only Sellers' *Indian* doctor (his nationality had been altered to accommodate what was still the actor's best-loved impersonation) succeeded in catching something of the original Shavian sparkle. La Loren was simply out of her depth, and the prestigious supporting cast, consisting of Alastair Sim, Vittorio de Sica (later to direct Sellers in a couple of films), Dennis Price and Gary Raymond, was disappointingly under-

Sophia Loren as *The Millionairess* proves th every man has his price

employed. One of the film's few amusing moments involved Sellers osculating Loren's heart, when the 'boompity-boompity-boompity-boom' rhythm which had been the record's refrain was heard, larger than life, on the soundtrack (though not, alas, set to music).

Notwithstanding the publicity surrounding the gilt-edged pairing of Loren and Sellers, *The Millionairess* had a mediocre commercial career both in England and the United States, and was lambasted by the critics. What made the experience a memorable one, however, was an element of which the publicity machine was as yet unaware: Sellers was falling in love with his leading lady. He had for several years been steadily drifting apart from Anne, who was also (but this he was only later to realize) drifting apart from him. For the first time in his career, he found himself partnering not only a star of truly international repute but one of the world's great beauties. And his liaison with her would certainly have come as a much needed boost to an ever hungry ego, as if the screen's most admired character actor (ironically forced by the plot demands of *The Millionairess* to appear insensitive to Loren's generous Neapolitan charms) had finally been permitted to play the romantic lead. It was probably more in the nature of a 'crush' than a deeply satisfying relationship: Loren was then, as she has remained, happily married to producer Carlo Ponti, a man possessed of even fewer matinée idol attributes than Sellers himself.

At the beginning, though it had become common knowledge around the set, he spoke to no one of the affair. Surprisingly, when at last in a confessional frame of mind – and in spite of being conscious that his infatuation could never be anything but fleeting – it was to Anne that he revealed all. As he admitted once in an interview: "I was responsible for the break-up of my marriage with Anne. If you fall in love with Sophia Loren and you chase around half of Europe for six months you can't expect your wife not to get upset." When, many years later, Loren published her intimate memoirs, he was both hurt and allegedly furious that she did not once deign to mention his name. "I do find that strange. After all, our relationship was one of the things that helped break up my first marriage. I was always rushing off to Italy to be with Sophia. It's odd that someone who apparently meant so much in her life – or so she said – should not figure in her life story. Still, perhaps she has her reasons."

Though he was at the top of his profession, in virtually every other respect it was an unhappy moment in Sellers' career. His father had always been a retiring man, less self-effacing than effaced by the seemingly inexhaustible energy of his wife and success of his son, neither of whom ever saw fit to seek his advice or take him into their confidence. In spite (maybe because) of this, Sellers was grief-stricken when he died in the winter of 1960, ominously enough of a heart attack; and for several months afterwards he was consumed with guilt over his lack of filial affection.

He peremptorily shifted the family out of Chipperfield, which was soon placed on the market, and into the lavish but impersonal surroundings of the Carlton Tower Hotel in London's Belgravia. His publicly stated reason for the abrupt move – "staff problems" – was uncharitably (but doubtless accurately) interpreted by gossip columnists as what might be termed 'distaff problems': Anne, he now learned, had fallen in love with a noted architect, Elias Levy. And the ambitious scheme which he was hatching with Mankowitz to form their own production company (its first project, to be directed by Sellers himself, was *Memoirs of a Cross-Eyed Man* with Diane Cilento) foundered in a morass of mutual recriminations and the least desirable type of publicity. At the same time, it was filtering through to the industry (especially after catastrophic trade figures in the United States) that *The Millionairess*, on which so many hopes had been pinned, was not about to make anyone connected with it a millionaire.

If one thing still seemed secure in this period of crisis, it was his personal popularity with moviegoers. But this too was to be dented by his next film, his first as a director. Part of the problem was the odd – not to say, inexplicable – choice of material. *Mr. Topaze* (optimistically retitled *I Love Money* for American release) was based on a long-running stage comedy by the French dramatist and filmmaker Marcel Pagnol, creator of the celebrated 'Marseilles trilogy', *Fanny*, *Marius* and *César*. Though it had been twice before brought to the screen (with, respectively, Louis Jouvet and Fernandel in the title role), its style and theme – a timorously idealistic schoolteacher, hired by a disreputable financier to sign checks and take the rap if necessary, catches on fast and ends up by appropriating both his boss's organization and his mistress – were rooted in prewar France and could have little appeal for youthful audiences in the frenetic '60s. Added to which, Sellers' direction of his fellow players (Nadia Gray, Herbert Lom, Leo McKern and Billie Whitelaw) proved as approximative as one might expect from a tyro with one eye on his own performance. Though not without a certain unassuming grace, *Mr. Topaze* finally seemed as shy and subdued as its hero, and did no business at all. On the credit side, one might mention some delicate period details and warm color photography.

Sellers followed his 'farewell début' as a director with a role and vehicle far more suited to his talents, that of Welsh librarian John Lewis in Sidney Gilliat's *Only Two Can Play*, a coarsely funny adaptation of the Kingsley Amis novel *That Uncertain Feeling*. Amis, one of the founding 'sons' of the angry young men movement, had, like Byron, become famous overnight with the publication of his satirical novel *Lucky Jim* (the film version of which, directed by the Boulting Brothers, unaccountably failed to feature Sellers) and this second work was very much in the same irreverent vein. The articulate Lewis rails against his pompous colleagues, his rapacious landlady and the suffocating, not-so-quiet desperation of his lower middle class existence. An unhoped for opportunity to transcend these dreary minutiae and dispense with the lubricious fantasies that he weaves around the local girls arises when he meets Elizabeth Gruffyd-Williams (Mai Zetterling), the glamorous Swedish-born wife of a local councillor. But their clumsy attempts at an affair in a romantically grand style are persistently frustrated (the inconvenient return of her husband, a cow peering through a car window). And when Lewis discovers that his promotion is due less to his own abilities than to her influence, he rebels against the situation and returns to his long-suffering wife (Virginia Maskell).

Whether gazing incredulously at the duck-patterned wallpaper of his drab lodgings or unsteadily toting his inamorata up to her satiny bedroom, Sellers vividly evoked the dilemma in which this "wan don who wanted to be a Don Juan" (as the *Time* reviewer put it) found himself. It was undoubtedly his bravura portrayal of middle class sexual harassment, plus the unaccustomed frankness of the love-making scenes, that caused the movie to become one of his biggest box-office hits to date. And perhaps vague hints here and there in the narrative of his own personal bed of nails gave the performance an edge of realistic despair it might otherwise have lacked. Almost as a form of therapy, Sellers soon after reprised his Indian doctor number as a guest star (along with Frank Sinatra, Dean Martin and David Niven) in *The Road to Hong Kong*, a last, doomed revival (by artificial respiration) of the '40s Hope-and-Crosby teaming.

Though he was now as well-known in the United States as at home and was later to live there in tax exile, he never fell in love with the country as so many of his compatriots had done. Selinger explained his lack of enthusiasm in this way: "After Peter's first visit to New York, he grumbled that no one there knew or cared who he was. They made him feel a nothing, a nobody. And when he returned a star and was greeted as such, well, he was revolted by what he saw as their hypocrisy. He was never happier than when just returned from America." Without ever having worked in Hollywood, he had made a handful of movies with American directors, actors or money (*tom thumb*, *The Mouse That Roared*, *The Millionairess*) and his next, Stanley Kubrick's *Lolita*, was no exception: in spite of boasting an American director, American settings and a predominantly American cast, it was filmed in England. It was, however, exceptional in every other respect, not least by offering Sellers what was perhaps his greatest ever role.

In *Lolita* he played Clare Quilty, poet and pervert, mentor of the heroine and tormentor of the hero, he of the twin names Humbert Humbert. Almost as if frankly to acknowledge that Quilty, who flits wraithlike through the novel's pages, has no existence beyond that of mere words, its author Vladimir Nabokov quotes a line in French from a play supposedly written by his character: "Ne manque pas de dire à ton amant, Chimène, comme le lac est beau car il faut qu'il t'y mène." ("Do not fail to tell your lover, Chimène, how beautiful the lake is for he really must take you there" – though not printed as such, it is in the original language an Alexandrine verse couplet.) "Qu'il t'y" – see the villain of the piece lurking behind that tongue-twisting French! So much publicity was expended on the drawbacks involved in casting the legendary nymphet herself that the equally tricky problem of unearthing a suitable screen incarnation of this phantasmagoric figure was somewhat obscured. To understand fully both the brilliance and inevitability of Kubrick's choice, one has only to peruse another page of the novel to read the following dialogue between Humbert Humbert and a disguised Quilty:

"Where the devil did you get her?"

"I beg your pardon?"

"I said: the weather is getting better."

"Seems so."

"Who's the lassie?"

"My daughter."

"You lie – she's not."

"I beg your pardon?"

"I said: July was hot."

Even without having seen the movie version, it would be difficult to read this Alice in Wonderland-like exchange and not hear with one's inner ear the inimitable Sellers inflections. He was a surprising yet obvious choice for the role and, in this supremely well cast movie, represents perhaps the greatest *coup* of all. Never has he more closely approached playing himself – or, at least, his persona as it was perceived by the public. In Lolita's bedroom, for example, we see pinned to the wall a cover portrait from one of Quilty's verse-reading records, which bears an uncanny resemblance to Sellers' own record sleeves. Quilty's disguises recall the impersonations Sellers used to perform on the variety stage (and indeed on record): as Dr. Zemf, the myopic college psychiatrist (almost a rehearsal for Strangelove), lasciviously outlining Lolita's charms "mit dem sving und dem jazz" or offering poor Humbert his last cigarette with an ungenerously literal "Keep ze pack"; as a slyly nervous policeman complimenting Humbert on his good fortune "I wish I had a lovely tall pretty small daughter like that. . ."; or, in the extraordinary opening sequence (the novel's climax), swathed in a dust-sheet, alcoholically befuddled and moaning softly in a Deep South accent when shot by Humbert "Gee, that hurt . . . that really hurt".

It was Sellers' finest hour (or two hours and a half). All those uncharitable criticisms that his performance unbalanced the movie are revealed or confirmed on a second viewing to be totally irrelevant, as his trio of co-stars were in no way overshadowed. James Mason's Humbert was, quite simply, an unforgettable creation, as he slavishly painted his little darling's toenails or reluctantly danced the cha cha cha with her mom, later remarking ambiguously to Lolita about a lunch prepared by the plump Shelley Winters "Your mother made a wonderful spread". Winters, wisely held in check by Kubrick, both touchingly and hilariously suggested emotional starvation in a framework of Kitschy middlebrow pretensions. And, notwithstanding the numerous critical cavils about her age (she was post-pubescent where the character as written was crucially pre-), Sue Lyon caught achingly well Lolita's blend of predatory gum-chewing vulgarity and quivering animal tenderness. If one has to find fault, it might be in Kubrick's decision (evidently out of economic considerations) to shoot the film in England, when much of the novel's velvety texture derives from the beady but beguiled eye it casts on the United States, and in black and white, when the novel's kaleidoscopic style positively cries out for garish Technicolor. Otherwise, one of the very few great Hollywood movies of the last twenty years.

Peter Sellers was back on top of the international bill. His professional dedication no less than his performance in *Lolita* had so impressed Kubrick that this demanding filmmaker, who rarely employs the same

...gmatic "Quilty" and
...." (Sue Lyon), at a high
school show—*Lolita* (1962).

actor twice, immediately invited him to play four separate roles – 'the lead and the lead and the lead and the lead' – in his projected 'Doomsday comedy', *Dr. Strangelove, or How I Learned To Stop Worrying And Love The Bomb*. After initial reluctance to become once more entangled with what he had come to feel was gimmicky multi-role playing, Sellers accepted. Since Kubrick is a scrupulously slow director, however, shooting on this A-rated farce about the H-Bomb did not start for another two years. Meanwhile, though the actor was suddenly swamped by lucrative offers from the United States, he preferred to retreat to the more modest dimensions offered by the domestic (in both senses of the word) product.

Waltz of the Toreadors (directed by John Guillermin) was a superficially stylish film version by Wolf Mankowitz of Jean Anouilh's play *La Valse des toréadors*, with the protagonist Général Saint-Pé anglicized into Fitzjohn. At its considerable best, Anouilh's work is distinguished by a flamboyant theatricality, a flair for subtle modulations within the same play between bitter and sweet (his comedies are often labeled either 'noires' or 'roses') and an obsession with innocence, generally personified by a virginal young heroine, sullied when forced into contact with a cynically egotistic world. Few of these qualities were visible in this hamfisted adaptation, whose director and screenwriter, visibly uncertain of the original work's appeal to movie audiences, had recourse to supposedly 'Gallic' romping between the General and whatever buxom servant-maid was at hand. The cast (Margaret Leighton as Fitzjohn's hysterical wife, John Fraser as his equerry, later revealed to be his son, and Dany Robin as the faithful Frenchwoman who arrives to exact a promise of marriage made seventeen years before) performed well beyond the call of duty. As the General, Sellers looked properly choleric in his uniform and walrus moustache, but sounded incongruously like Major Bloodnok of *The Goon Show*. Which is to say that he was often extremely funny, but in a tone that undermined the fragility of Anouilhesque tragi-comedy. The movie was graced by an effervescent score (including the naggingly catchy title waltz) by Richard Addinsell.

Waltz of the Toreadors made money, but the wave of success that Sellers appeared to be riding again was part of a tide that would ebb as well as flow. The pathos of James Hill's *The Dock Brief*, in which he played the eccentric, incompetent barrister Morgenhall, proved too modest and slight to attract much attention at the box-office. It had started life as a television play by John Mortimer (a barrister himself) and a small-scale television play is basically what it remained. Set principally in a detention cell (though the movie, to doubtful effect, opted for 'opening out' the action by means of superfluous flashbacks), it told the story of Morgenhall's brief to defend Fowle (Richard Attenborough), a seedy seed merchant, on the charge of murdering his wife. To his astonishment, Fowle cheerfully admits to the crime and, in the lonely intimacy of the cell, the two men map out an elaborate argument that must surely save the

defendant from the gallows. When in court, however, the barrister finds himself abruptly bereft of all his oratorical *élan* and the case for the defence quickly collapses. In an ironic coda, we discover that the judgment against Fowle has been quashed on the grounds that he had been inadequately defended; and, though both men are quite aware of the sadder truth, he congratulates Morgenhall on the cunning of his tactics.

In an interview given to *The Sunday Times* just following the announcement of Sellers' death, Mortimer recounts the circumstances in which the actor eased his way into the role: "For a long time he couldn't decide how to play Morgenhall; but the day before shooting was due to start he ordered cockles at lunchtime in Shepperton Studios. The shellfish came with a whiff of the sea and the memory of Morecambe, and brought the idea of a faded North Country accent and the suggestion of a scrappy moustache. He had been thrown the lifeline of a voice, and work could begin."

That year he made two other British movies. The first, *Heavens Above!*, may be seen as a pendant to the Boulting Brothers' earlier series of comedies tilting at such Establishment institutions as the army, the law, the universities, the diplomatic service and industry. Nothing remained but religion. Unfortunately, it soon became clear that neither Sellers nor the producer-director twins could call on any extensive experience of the inner mechanism of the Anglican church, and the intended satire rapidly descended into smutty, mean-spirited sarcasm demeaning to everyone and everything it touched upon. Sellers (as the Reverend John Smallwood) tumbling into an open grave on his way to a church council meeting, a mongrel urinating against his leg as he stands dejectedly in the rain, the steward announcing to a brace of bishops in a railway compartment "Last supper now being served!" – these are a few random examples of the movie's self-styled anti-clerical 'wit'.

Even more offensive, however, was its supposedly 'liberal' treatment of a local black dustman (played by Brock Peters), who chants traditional Anglican hymns as if they were Negro spirituals and whose dialogue consists almost solely of quaint Uncle Tomish lines, e.g. speaking of the church congregation, he refers to them as "Packed tight together like seeds in a melon!" The middle classes are shown to be uniformly dotty and ultra-conservative, the lower orders (in particular, a family of squatters whom Smallwood befriends) irredeemably scruffy and ungrateful. The narrative ends, in desperation, with Smallwood packed off in a rocket and belting out hymns over the galaxy, with an American commentator predictably exclaiming at take-off, "Holy smoke!"

Sellers himself struggled in vain with the difficult role of a naively decent man who has failed to think through the problems of Christian goodness at odds with the twentieth century. But here, patently, he had 'lost his voice'. Unlike Kite, his characterization of Smallwood, with beatific smile and unfashionably wavy hair, did not give the impression of being the fruit of long and patient observation: throughout the film, he remains curiously undefined, out of focus, neither an individual nor an instantly recognizable type. Goodness is, of course, a notoriously ticklish concept for an actor to express and, though he made a brave stab at it, one can only feel that his gallery of rogues carries far greater conviction. Typically, however, he made the most of the occasionally sharp lines of dialogue that came his way, as when he gently castigates his aristocratic benefactress, Lady Despard (Isabel Jeans), for her businesslike approach to the Trinity: "The way you talk, you'd think the Father, Son and Holy Ghost was a firm of builder's merchants." The supporting cast featured Cecil Parker, Ian Carmichael, Eric Sykes and Bernard Miles.

As its title suggests, *The Wrong Arm of the Law* (directed by Cliff Owen) was yet another of those bobbies 'n' robbers farces which Sellers, in spite of his flourishing international reputation, was still being offered in England. The perfunctory but serviceable plot involved an amalgama-

ader "Pearly Gates"
trates with "Inspector
Parker" (Lionel
as henchman "Siggy
tz" (Tutte Lemkov)
join in – *Wrong Arm*
aw (1963).

tion of criminals and police to bring about the downfall of a trio of upstart Australians who were upsetting the status quo by arriving on the scene of a crime disguised as policemen and making off with the 'honest' crook's hard-earned booty. Thanks to brisk, no-nonsense direction, nice performances all round and a script that managed to squeeze a few new ideas out of a tube that one would have supposed long since emptied – an underworld conference conducted along trade union lines, a meeting between Scotland Yard and the criminal fraternity at Battersea Fun Fair, Sellers as gang leader Pearly Gates doubling as a French couturier in an exclusive Bond Street salon – the film proved consistently funny and, though hardly testing his abilities to the full, nothing that its star need feel ashamed of.

Perhaps in a confused attempt to forget the traumas of his private life (in January 1963 he had petitioned for divorce on the grounds of Anne's adultery with Levy and a *decree nisi* was granted three months later), he was bustling from film to film, from disguise to disguise, without ever pausing to reflect on where his career might be leading him.

It's quite probable that many of the younger moviegoers who have made the Pink Panther series the most commercially successful cycle of comedies in the history of the cinema, or who have giggled at the animated antics of the cartoon Panther himself, might never guess the precise relationship between that sleek urban jungle cat and the bumbling, accident-prone Inspector Clouseau of the Sureté (whose name no doubt derives from that of the celebrated French director of pseudo-Hitchcockian thrillers, H.-G. Clouzot). Unless one had seen the original movie, entitled simply *The Pink Panther*, one might be excused for not knowing that the Panther was actually a diamond, a priceless gem inherited by an Indian princess and coveted by half the jewel thieves in Europe. It acquired its bizarre name because of a faint pink glow just visible at its center, which in the movie's credit titles materialized into its zoological equivalent.

Blake Edwards' comedy wove a criminal and romantic imbroglio around the gem's owner, Princess Dala (Claudia Cardinale), an international arch-thief 'the Phantom', alias Sir Charles Willingham (David Niven), his rascally nephew George (Robert Wagner), the zealous but incompetent Clouseau (Sellers) and his icy, statuesque wife who is working in league with the Phantom (Capucine). The movie, boasting an enchanting theme tune by Henry Mancini and some colorful traveloguish décors in Paris, Rome and Cortina d'Ampezzo, promised to be a smooth, chic comedy-thriller, none too taxing on the intelligence.

What raised it above that modest ambition, however, was Sellers' performance as Jacques Clouseau. Here he could indulge his craving for purely physical, Keaton-inspired humor and he seized the opportunity with both hands (and two left feet). Clouseau is the kind of person incapable of crossing a room without leaving shattered furniture in his wake; and though slapstick can become tiresomely repetitive unless a disciplined balance is struck between comic invention and anarchic destruction, the best moments of this (and, though less frequently, its sequels) involved gags so original yet so elementary that they have come to be associated exclusively with its maladroit hero. Clouseau nonchalantly resting his hand on a large globe of the world without realising that it is spinning; Clouseau saluting a superior without realizing that he is holding a truncheon in his hand; Clouseau imperiously raising his index finger without realizing that someone's nostril is exactly situated to receive it. "Without realizing" – these are the key words, as all of Clouseauesque comedy is based on the notion of someone automatically making the gestures expected of him while failing to take into consideration the possibility that others – both humans and objects – might at that moment be inhabiting the same limited space.

In fact, the character provides a classic demonstration of Bergsonian comedy – the comedy of rigidity from which a fall invariably ensues. To which should be added the influence of cartoon violence familiar from the Tom and Jerry and Road Runner series (an influence in Edwards' work even without Sellers, e.g. *The Great Race*). Clouseau would generally reappear on the screen without any visible scar to show for the multiple catastrophes which had befallen him in the preceding scene.

The's up for Capucine, seau" strikes for the e – *The Pink Panther*

But he did not completely relinquish his genius for mimicry. With his tightly belted trench coat, sporty tweed hat, Ronald Colman moustache and Holmesian magnifying glass, Clouseau seemed something of a cartoon himself (and indeed was turned into one for a children's TV show). Sellers also encumbered him with an outrageously precious French accent that even his *French* colleagues at the Sureté have difficulty in deciphering. The word 'phone', for example, would emerge from his prissily pursed lips as 'phön' (approximating it 'phönetically') and 'monkey' something like 'minké'.

With the movie's success assured, Edwards at once proposed a sequel, to which Sellers, who had found the experience of working with him euphoric, readily agreed. Moviemaking enabled him to subsume his own increasing personal isolation in teamwork. He had not yet moved out of his sumptuous Hampstead penthouse (which was ironically the cause of Anne meeting Elias Levy, its designer) and into the 400-pounds-a-week Oliver Messel suite at the Dorchester Hotel, the first of a series of blandly luxurious residences whose only personal stamp would be the clutter of gadgets – photography, hi-fi, games – strewn over the ankle-deep carpets. Anne married Levy, and it was amicably agreed that the children be brought up by them. Staying on in the empty Hampstead apartment, with all its memories, seemed to reveal a masochistic, self-pitying streak in Sellers' nature, and his valet of many years standing, Bert Mortimer, was genuinely concerned that he might try to kill himself. Penthouses, after all, are made for suicidal leaps.

His loneliness was only intensified by the number of beautiful women who were passing through his life, whom he escorted to premières or parties. He was chronically insecure, persuaded that it was his name alone that could attract the opposite sex. Yet fame and wealth apart – and genius, than which nothing has more potent sex appeal – he was still, by most standards, a physically desirable man, with unnaturally intense eyes that could magnetize the person in their gaze. And when on form, he knew how to be a charming and amusing companion. Anyone less vulnerable would have taken for granted that many of London's eligible beauties were flattered to be seen (and photographed) at his side. It was at this period that he embarked on a series of compulsive crash diets designed to transform a pleasantly plump young man into an oddly frail middle-aged one. He also began to sport somberly tinted glasses – not, as with certain film stars, to attract attention, but genuinely to protect the anonymity which remained, he felt, at the core of his personality. Sellers, in short, could be described as a famous man inside whom an unknown was screaming to get out.

After a project which came to nothing – an adaptation by John Mortimer of Robert Graves' novel *I, Claudius* in which Sellers (like Charles Laughton before him and, on television, Derek Jacobi after him) would play the title role of the stuttering, epileptic Emperor – he began to immerse himself in the difficult gestation of Kubrick's *Dr. Strangelove*. For the three performances he gave in this movie he was to receive perhaps the warmest accolades of his whole professional life, and there were some who would feel that he had been unjustly denied an Oscar (or three) for the most brilliant quick-change act in cinema history. Undoubtedly, he was at the very peak of his career. The trouble with being at such a peak, however, is that everywhere one looks the only direction possible would seem to be down. . . .

4 A Thousand Voices – And Nine Lives

4

4

4

4

STANLEY KUBRICK'S *Dr. Strangelove or How I Learned To Stop Worrying And Love The Bomb* (loosely based on Peter George's novel *Red Alert*) is a grim fairy tale whose introductory phrase might be, not 'Once upon a time . . .' but 'What if . . .' What if, for example, an insane US Army General were to run amok, initiating a B-52 attack on the Soviet Union? What if he were to commit suicide before divulging the code by which the bombers could be recalled? What if, when that code had somehow been deciphered, one of the planes were attacked by the Russians and its radio communications equipment destroyed? And what if the Russians themselves had constructed the ultimate atomic weapon, a 'Doomsday' machine, impossible to defuse in the event of a nuclear attack and calculated to raze the entire planet? The only conceivable answer to that series of not-so-hypothetical questions provides the movie with its dénouement and, in a sense, its QED: mushroom clouds billow gracefully over a depopulated planet while the saccharine voice of Vera Lynn sings, from some heavenly BBC studio, the World War II (now III) ballad 'We'll meet again. . . .'

The movie offers a relentless exposition – step by step, as in a countdown – of the strict, inflexible logic of unreason, and its warning is perhaps even more urgently timely today than when it was made back in 1963. Shot in black and white photography that is either glittering (as in Ken Adam's spectacular War Room set in the Pentagon) or hand-held and grainy (the attack by National Guardsmen on Burpelson air base), *Dr. Strangelove* is in narrative terms black through and through. Here 'white'

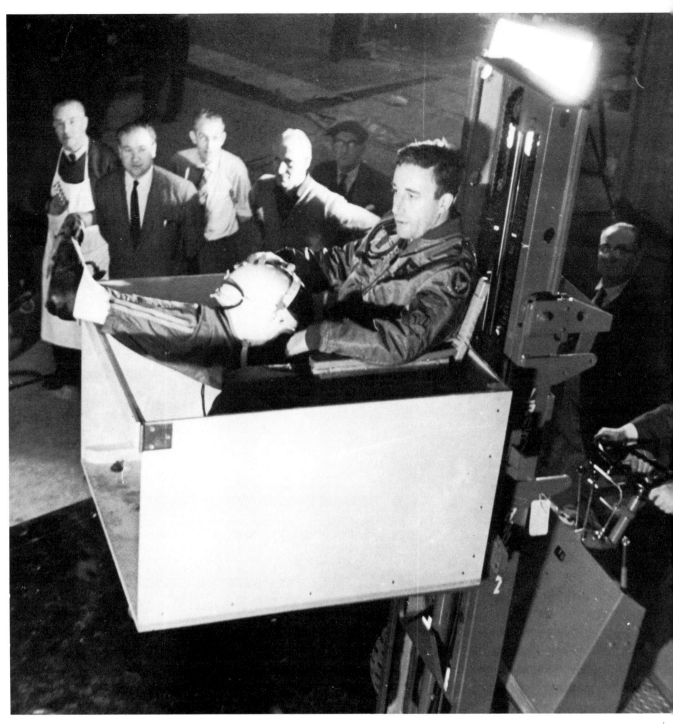

The part he did not play
Dressed as "Major 'King'
Kong" – *Dr. Strangelove*
(1963).

is either illusory or restricted to action well above the earth, e.g. in the
credit sequence where, to the ironic strains of 'Try a Little Tenderness',
the fueling of the B-52s is conceived as a balletic copulation. In fact, a
current of sexual symbolism is perceptible throughout the whole movie,
from the paranoid fears of General Jack D. Ripper (Sterling Hayden) that
the Russians have polluted "our precious bodily fluids", thereby interfer-
ing with his sexual prowess, to the moment when Major 'King' Kong
(Slim Pickens) hurtles to cheerful destruction astride an atomic bomb

which has become, between his legs, the world's most potent and grandiose phallus.

Kong was one of the roles assigned to Sellers by Kubrick. But during
the movie's preparatory stages he had enormous difficulties finding first
the voice and, by a familiar progression, the rest of the character. It was
the British actress Janette Scott, with whom he was having an affair more
serious than most (there was even, briefly, talk of marriage), who, dis-
turbed by the intensity of his frustration, advised him against tackling it.
As it happened, he broke his ankle and Kubrick was obliged to replace
him with the excellent Pickens. So Sellers played 'only' Group Captain
Lionel Mandrake, an archetypal English RAF officer who manages to
decode the ravings doodled on a scratch pad by the mad Ripper, President Mervin Muffley and the sinister Strangelove himself.

What is astonishing about this triple achievement is precisely the
extent to which it was 'triple'. Kubrick's reassurance to the actor that the
feat, if brought off, would represent much more than a gimmick was
triumphantly vindicated. Contrary to his work in *The Mouse That Roared*
(or even Guinness's impersonations in *Kind Hearts and Coronets*), one
was rarely conscious of the virtuoso aspect of an actor giving three
separate performances in a single movie: he appeared to be three separate
actors. There seemed to be no real behavioral relation between Mandrake
and Muffley, for example, beyond the fact that both were ineffectual
milksops in positions of authority. Mandrake's hyperdeveloped sense of
the proprieties – as evidenced by his gentle cajoling of Ripper when
sterner tactics were called for – is defeated only by Colonel 'Bat' Guano
(Keenan Wynn) who, obsessed with what he calls "*preverts*", dutifully
tries to prevent him from destroying Army property: in this instance, a
Coca Cola machine from which a dime might be illegally extracted, a
telephone call made to the White House and the world saved from
extinction. Muffley – small, bald and entirely lacking in Presidential
charisma – is persistently bypassed by events, whether they are reported
to him by General Buck Turgidson (George C. Scott) who, offended by the
President's criticism of a system that appears to be heading for a global
holocaust, protests, "I don't think it's fair to condemn a whole program
because of a single slip-up", or in the final hours of humanity by
Strangelove himself. He is well-meaning but bewildered, still determined at the very last to placate his tipsy Soviet counterpart on the 'hot
line': "No, you couldn't be sorrier than I am, Dmitri. . . ."

But the most audacious stroke of all is undoubtedly the Doctor. Only at
the very end of the movie (and the world) are we allowed to see him
properly, with his crinkled wavy coiffure and maniacally glinting eyes,
as though he were an exclusively nocturnal creature positively thriving
on reveries of apocalypse. His artificial metal arm jerks involuntarily into
ill-timed Nazi salutes or clamps itself firmly around his throat. He revels
with guttural gusto at the prospect of spending his post-nuclear existence

surrounded by a harem of generously endowed young women, all conscientiously propagating the species. And his apotheosis – rising triumphantly from his wheelchair with the demented cry "Mein Führer, I can valk!" – coincides with the final catastrophe. Strangelove is perhaps a caricature – but a caricature of genius.

Three great performances in a great film. Sellers would have been forgiven for wanting to take a break, but he now seemed to have become a fully paid-up member of Workaholics Anonymous (or Famous). Not that the two movies which he completed in the months that followed could have been too exerting for him. *The World of Henry Orient* (based on the novel by Nora Johnson) was a light-fantastic comedy directed by a relative newcomer, George Roy Hill, who would later achieve celebrity with such blockbusters as *Butch Cassidy and the Sundance Kid* and *The Sting*. It revolved around the romantic fantasies of two teenage girls in New York (ravishingly photographed by Boris Kaufman) when they attach themselves to a mediocre concert painist called Henry Orient. A pleasant, eminently forgettable movie, it did at least give Sellers the opportunity to indulge in some rakish clowning at the keyboard and, with the underrated Paula Prentiss, in the bedroom.

Blake Edwards' *A Shot in the Dark* attempted to insert Clouseau into the framework of a French Boulevard farce by Marcel Achard, which had already been adapted for Broadway by Harry Kurnitz. But the character had not yet generated sufficient dynamic to carry a whole movie, as was the case – whatever one felt about them – with the later sequels, whose titles all began with what had become almost a logo "The Pink Panther. . .". The jet-setting glamor and starry cast of the original were sorely missed: it was filmed for the most part in the studio. Moreover, the coarsening of Clouseau's humor made this film, for Sellers-watchers, considerably less satisfying than its predecessor, not only in the excessive number of gags which involved his falling fully clothed into rivers or ornamental ponds (or being trapped stark naked in his car with the similarly exposed Elke Sommer), but also in the introduction of a sado-masochistic relationship with his long-suffering superior at the Sureté, Inspector Dreyfus, played by Herbert Lom as a one-man orgy of tics and twitches. The basic problem with *A Shot in the Dark* was that its reduced budget did not permit the kind of expensive location shooting of the first, while neither Sellers nor Edwards had exactly hit on the format within which Clouseau could blossom forth as an autonomous hero. It was also notable in that relations between them, so idyllic during their first collaboration, were now rather strained, as Sellers, after his inconclusive experience with *Mr. Topaze*, was beginning to acquire the unpopular reputation of a 'back seat' director.

Though *A Shot in the Dark* was a success, no immediate plans were entertained to extend the series. In 1964, both Sellers and Edwards were (or appeared to be) at the height of their careers and hardly felt the need to

onies of the artist –
orld of Henry Orient

eau'' explains the art
lling the bent cue – A
the Dark (1964).

The "Inspector" shocke[d]
rigid at the sight of a sca[ntily]
clad Elke Sommer – *A S[hot in]
the Dark* (1964).

play safe. A decade later, however, things would look a little different for both of them.

Sellers was now ensconced in the Dorchester Hotel where it was that, in the lobby, he first caught sight of a small, wide-eyed, elfin blonde buying magazines from the bookstand. His reaction was not dissimilar to that when Selinger introduced him to Anne: if not love, then sexual attraction at first sight. He was instantly smitten. As quickly and decently as he could, he made inquiries as to her identity. She was Britt Ekland, a Swedish starlet who had just signed up to play in Twentieth Century-Fox's *The Guns at Batasi*. Since his favorite medium, Maurice Woodruff, had six months before predicted that his second wife's initials would be B.E., it was almost as if they were meeting by appointment. On occasion, of course, such predictions all but force their credulous subjects to will them to come true, but a man as sensitive to extra-sensory phenomena could hardly help but be impressed by the coincidence.

In the next few days, despite continuing to delude himself with the notion that a reconciliation was still possible with Anne, who was already expecting a baby by Levy, the image of this (as he imagined) Nordic virgin preyed on his mind and dreamily impractical ideas even crossed it. Arranging for her to be flown over at his expense from New York, for example, where she had gone to meet with Fox executives. Finally, discovering that she had returned to the Dorchester, he dispatched Bert to her room with the proposal that his master, Peter Sellers, take some photographs of her. Though, as she recalls, she had just emerged from the shower to answer the door, she was determined that this would be no come-as-you-are session and wore the most demurely unrevealing costume she could unearth from her closet. Sellers, apparently unperturbed, treated her with a purely professional courtesy, only slightly betrayed by uncharacteristic nervousness. The session over, he whisked her off in his outsize American limousine to see *The Pink Panther*, which was playing in London's West End at the time. The evening ended in his suite, but this time around – at least, according to her kiss-and-tell autobiography *True Britt* – it was to be 'No Sex, Please, I'm Britt' (and for Sellers, perhaps, 'Shut Your Eyes and Think of Ekland').

In the following weeks, to mix metaphors hideously, the ice melted and began to snowball. He proposed to her, appropriately enough, by Telstar and on her return from another trip to the States they were married in a Guildford registrar's office with his cronies from the good old days of Grafton's pub, David Lodge and Graham Stark, as best men. Their marriage was not one of love and certainly not of convenience, but of sexual satisfaction. Sellers' friends were apprehensive about the whimsically whirlwind nature of their courtship, but neither Peg nor the bride's family had any strenuous objections. It was, in fact, from Sellers himself that surfaced the first tell-tale cracks in their relationship.

Possibly because he realized that his hold over Britt had never been consummated *by love* on either side (possibly, too, out of an unformulated disenchantment at the indubitable fact that she proved less virginal than he had childishly supposed), he became almost immediately a victim to jealousy. He shuddered at the thought of her shooting *Guns at Batasi* alone in Pinewood Studios just outside London, while he was in Hollywood embroiled in the aptly titled *Kiss Me, Stupid* for Billy Wilder. He worried about the studio boss, a twentieth century fox himself, that notorious womanizer and Tsar of the casting couch, Darryl F. Zanuck. He wondered what the F. stood for. Every evening, telephoning Britt from across a continent and an ocean, Sellers would imperceptibly switch the tenor of their conversation from inquiring about her work to interrogating her as to whom she had spoken to that day, who she was dining with, etc. Taking an instant dislike – by proxy, as it were, for they had never met – to her leading man, John Leyton, he bombarded her with gifts, phone calls and, on one occasion, by three successive telegrams, each bearing a single word: 'I', 'Love' and 'You'.

The crisis came at Easter. Michael and Sarah were joining their father for the holiday period, but Sellers wanted Britt. At Pinewood, a four day recess from shooting was planned; having asked for it to be extended in her case, she met with a flat refusal. But Sellers would not be discouraged by such a piffling detail. He arranged for a limousine to collect her almost clandestinely from the studio and smuggle her off to Heathrow. Twelve hours later, she arrived in Los Angeles without luggage but astonished to discover that, in the Beverly Hills mansion which he had rented (ironically, from the then President of Twentieth Century-Fox, Spyros Skouras), the ample closets were stuffed full of just her style in clothes, shoes and lingerie.

Rashly, Britt stayed on. Writs were served on both of them, and Sellers found himself eventually obliged to pay Fox over 60,000 dollars to cover the expense caused by his wife's walking out on a movie whose shooting was already underway, a clear case of breach of contract. But such an irritation hardly impinged on the lovers' happiness in each other's company. This was to be their honeymoon. And to up the ante, they had begun to make use of amyl nitrate capsules as aids to sexual endurance. It was after one such bout of deceptively intense love making that Sellers suddenly complained of agonizing chest pains and mild paralysis in one arm. Convinced he had suffered a heart attack (and equally convinced it was hereditary), he told Britt at once to telephone his physician, Dr. Rex Kennamer. Early next morning, he was transferred to the Cedars of Lebanon Hospital to undergo a series of tests. If heart attack it had been, however, it appeared at the moment to have been a mild one. Britt informed United Artists, the company producing *Kiss Me, Stupid*, of her husband's unavailability. Sellers was not noticeably popular among his fellow performers; and with the romantic (but costly) defection of Britt from *Guns at Batasi* still in everyone's mind, it was natural that not a few uncharitably put his condition down to a severe case of temperament.

Sellers was advised to spend the night in the hospital for further tests. Rather reluctantly he agreed, suggesting to Britt that the children need not be troubled over such a minor matter. Ominously, however, at five o'clock the next morning, the telephone began to ring in the mansion. It was answered by Bert the valet. A few moments later, he tapped on Britt's door with the news that her husband's condition had crucially deteriorated. Her presence was urgently requested at his bedside. When they arrived half-an-hour later, Sellers, pale and somehow shrunken, was scarcely visible beneath the sinister undergrowth of tubes, drip feeds, oxygen equipment and the Pacemaker machine that was understudying his heart. They learned that at 2.30am his attendant nurse had summoned the house doctor upon finding her patient unconscious, bereft of both pulse and blood pressure. The job of resuscitation began on the instant and continued until, with painful slowness, his 'dead' body shuddered into life again — sufficiently so, at least, for him to be moved to the hospital's Intensive Care Unit. He had had no fewer than *seven* coronaries in the space of two hours and just one more, however mild, would prove fatal. His chance of surviving through the night was rated at one in ten.

As everyone knows, Peter Sellers did not die in 1964. The man of so many faces and voices also appeared to have been gifted with more than the regulation number of lives. Gradually, very gradually, he emerged from the cottonwool cocoon of a four-day coma. His heart and pulse fluttered back to their regular rhythm. When he started making tetchily impatient calls to agents and producers, it was evident that he intended to be with us for some time to come. Newspaper offices all over the world hastily replaced his obituary in the so-called 'Morgue' file, friends and colleagues put away their glowing personal testimonies as it was at last revealed to Sellers himself that, technically, he had died eight times, a record that only a cat can match. Bizarrely, though he never made public any personal anecdote concerning his own brief sojourn in limbo, Sellers retained an unshakable conviction in the powers of the dead to communicate with the living.

Such close proximity to death necessitated fully six months of recuperation, taking photographs, riding his bicycle and practising a new fad of his, archery. Even so, it was with considerable chagrin that he learned of his replacement, on *Kiss Me, Stupid*, by the American comic actor, Ray Walston. (Incidentally, the movie – co-starring Kim Novak and Dean Martin – proved to be a pungent distillation of Wilder's most bittersweet manner, and was much undervalued by both the critics and public of the period.) How else can one justify the unguarded remarks about the Hollywood community that he made to reporters on his return to England, subsequently sharpening and amplifying them in an interview with the movie critic of the London *Evening Standard*, Alexander Walker? "America I would go back to gladly tomorrow, but as far as film-land is concerned I've taken the round trip for good. The noise and, to coin a phrase, the people. At the studios they give you every creature comfort except the satisfaction of being able to get the best work out of yourself." Sellers complained of interference on the set, of having to kowtow to visiting relatives of the studio brass. He painted a sour picture of a serious artist plagued with philistines and hangers-on.

The article, speedily relayed to Hollywood, provoked from the cast and director of *Kiss Me, Stupid* an immediate reaction. A telegram (mysteriously released to the international press) was dispatched to the recuperating Sellers. Its five words conveyed a chilling terseness that could not totally be attributed to the stylistic limitations of telegraphese. "Talk about unprofessional rat finks" was all it said. Though Sellers was sufficiently hurt (and also perhaps conscious of having committed a grave tactical error) to defend his comments in a full-page advertisement in *Variety*, paying particular tribute to the staff of Cedars of Lebanon Hospital, this summary rejection by his fellow performers seemed to exacerbate an already visible tendency to introversion. He became ever more touchy, ruthless and unapproachable; and Britt, whose infatuation had been transformed into genuine love by the whole nerve-wracking ordeal, was henceforth required to be at one and the same time wife, mistress, mother, secretary and nurse. But Spike Milligan offered another, curious view on what had happened, related to the death of Sellers' father: "Years before he had this heart attack he always worried about it, was always searching for the bloody thing as if it were a letter that he knew had been posted and hadn't arrived."

All that remained of Sellers' illness was an itch – the itch to return to work as soon as possible. Since in his *Variety* ad he had claimed that in America "regrettably the creative side in me couldn't accept the sort of conditions under which work had to be carried out", Hollywood appeared to be out of bounds – at least, until his 'betrayal' was forgiven him. As a compromise, he flew over to New York to play a minor guest role with Britt in a UNO television documentary 'A Carol For Another Christmas' (it was also about this time that his flat was robbed of 20,000 pounds worth of valuables, an excuse for him to install the most sophisticated burglar-alarm gadgetry on the market). But his participation demanded only three days' shooting, and he was increasingly eager to tackle a full-scale role (or roles) in a major movie.

Producer Charles Feldman offered him that of a manic German psychiatrist, Dr. Fritz Fassbender, in his new Franco-American co-production, *What's New, Pussycat?*, to be directed by Clive Donner. Britt, who was now pregnant, joined him in Paris, where the baby, a girl whom they named Victoria, was born. In a sense, *Pussycat* ends a phase in Sellers' career that was launched by *The Ladykillers*: where in the latter he was paired with an actor, Alec Guinness, whom he eventually replaced as the leading figure in British comedy, he now found himself co-starring with the movie's scenarist who would shortly become the most adulated comedian in international cinema, Woody Allen. Allen's script, studded with variously amusing one-liners, involved an English playboy and editor of a fashion magazine (Peter O'Toole at his most coyly ethereal) whose attentions to his fiancée (Romy Schneider) are constantly distracted by the entourage of leggy models at his office. Ill-advisedly, he consults Fassbender, who is not without marital problems of his own. And that, basically, completes the narrative: what follows can most charitably be defined as 'complications'.

Unless one were totally averse to anything smacking of the 'Swinging Sixties', however, the movie seemed to promise well: a cast that also included Capucine, Paula Prentiss and Ursula Andress, a catchy Burt Bacharach theme song and glittering credit titles in updated Art Nouveau style by the British animator Richard Williams (whose inventive cartoonery would provide almost the only bright moments in the later *Pink Panther* instalments). But after an inspired opening gag – when Fassben-

d me woman, or I'll
elf'. "Fritz
der" threatens his
na (Edra Gale) –
New Pussycat?

der's Wagnerian wife, suspecting adultery, bellows "Is she prettier than
me?", Sellers, with a familiar gargle of incredulity, retorts "Is she prettier
than you? *I'm* prettier than you!" – the promise was instantly broken. The
quartet of leading ladies were given disastrously little to do; Allen,
though touching, had visibly not yet found his stride as a screen performer; and O'Toole's sense of farce contrived to be both airy and flat-
footed.

   In a Baby Jane fright wig and a collection of velveteen jackets, Sellers
managed to save a few moments, especially when Allen's script caught
an authentic whiff of Goonish lunacy. A bewildered O'Toole to Sellers in
the Crazy Horse Saloon nightclub: "If you followed me, how did you
arrive here before me?" Sellers, defensively: "I followed you . . . very
fast." Or Sellers learnedly outlining his theory of sexual psychology: "A

le role in Dr.
love (1963). "Group
Mandrake" . . .

sident Mervin
" . . .

"Dr. Strangelove"

lascivious adulterer is a man who is . . . a lascivious adulterer." But it's the kind of movie during which one cannot help but feel that the performers are having a much more enjoyable time than the audience (a feeling that kills any desire to laugh *at* them). Or where, if the screenwriter has run out of ideas, the director simply resorts to putting all the cast into go-carts or bringing on Richard Burton for a brief guest appearance (greeted by O'Toole with a nonchalant "Give my love to what's her name"). Like the '60s themselves, these high jinks have dated badly.

Yet it was a huge hit and Sellers, now firmly back in his stride, immediately began preparing for a cameo role in Bryan Forbes' adaptation of Robert Louis Stevenson and Lloyd Osbourne's masterpiece of black comedy, *The Wrong Box*, with John Mills, Ralph Richardson, Michael Caine, Peter Cook and Dudley Moore, Nanette Newman, Tony Hancock and Wilfrid Lawson. Once again, the credit titles proved oddly revealing of the scope of the movie's ambitions; in stylish Art Nouveau designs, they unerringly (and unwittingly) succeeded in pinning down what had gone awry with the conception envisioned by Forbes and his American screenwriters, Larry Gelbart and Burt Shevelove. Rather than any real endeavor, however crude, to reconstruct the visual and verbal textures of Victorian England, the movie opted for a '60s romp in cod Victoriana, very much in the manner of Lester's *Help!* and certain Carnaby Street boutiques of the period (e.g. 'I was Lord Kitchener's Valet'). Though the unique whimsy of the original novel positively ached for film treatment, Forbes' version was too frantically slapdash and gag-hungry to capitalize even on what seeemed most obviously cinematic in print. With such a cast, of course, it would be difficult to make a movie entirely lacking in comic distinction; and Sellers' crooked doctor, festooned with cats which he distractedly employs as napkins, blotters and pillows, was a marvellous, all too fleeting 'turn' which momentarily galvanized the proceedings into a semblance of wit. A sadly wasted opportunity.

Given the brevity of Sellers' performance, the fact that *The Wrong Box* turned out to be a costly flop would not have caused him many sleepless nights. But his increasingly unreliable taste was more dramatically highlighted by his next choice of director and movie, Vittorio de Sica's *After the Fox*, to be shot in Italy. He had long been an admirer of the Italian director. But de Sica's work had catastrophically declined since his neo-realist movies in the '40s and '50s – most notably, *Bicycle Thieves* and *Umberto D*. And why, in any case, he should have been considered a suitable director for a Neil Simon-scripted heist caper *à la Topkapi* is just one of the impenetrable mysteries of international movie 'packaging'.

This, one of his most dismal efforts, could well have been entitled 'Gold Bullion Thieves'. It involved the ingenious plan of a down at the heel Italian swindler, Aldo Vanucci (Sellers), to disguise the clandestine arrival of stolen bullion on Italian soil by passing himself off as a movie director and persuading the populace (and police) of a small fishing

rector "Aldo
i" oversees the
of the consignment
oullion – *After the*
56).

village to participate in the making of . . . a heist movie. Somewhere
lurked the germ of a real comic idea, but it was unceremoniously buried
under the frantic mugging of almost all concerned, the incongruity of
Simon's one-liners in a *Carry On* context and, especially, de Sica's wit-
less and offensive attempts to parody cinematic styles including his own
("What's neo-realism?" someone asks, to be told "No money."). The few
witty lines – de Sica as himself directing a Biblical epic shouts to an
assistant "I want more sand on the desert!" – and fewer original situations – it is Vanucci, comfortably installed in prison, who offers his
visiting family fruit, cigarettes and a chicken, rather than vice-versa – are
quickly offset by the director's bold ignorance of such a thing as comic
timing.

As for the performers, little need be said. Sellers displayed an occasional spark of his old self, but his impersonations – a moustachioed
carabiniere, a priest absent-mindedly blessing a passer-by on the Via
Veneto – were no more than tired variations on ultra-familiar themes. He
was beginning to repeat himself. Britt, his co-star and a brunette for the
occasion, was a pleasant blob on the screen. Only Akim Tamiroff as Okra,

the mastermind behind the robbery (and self-styled inventor of 'Okra-scope'), and Victor Mature as a wrinkle-conscious ham actor on the skids emerged with their reputations anything like intact (even, in Mature's case, enhanced).

It's difficult to imagine, given the extraordinarily misguided notion of a Sellers-de Sica-Simon collaboration, how *After the Fox* could ever have worked. But its quite startling degree of ineptness no doubt also derived from the squalid maneuvering that took place behind the scenes – most of it by Sellers himself. Though it had been his initial enthusiasm for de Sica which got the project off the ground, there was a fundamental incompatibility in their approaches to filmmaking that could only result in a collision. The actor rarely cared to admit it, but he required a kind of benevolent friction – or, like an athlete, a sense of competition – from his director before he could start to hone his performance into a fully rounded and believable character composition. Left to his own devices, well, that was all he was left with – devices. The mimic's bag of tics.

Even apart from the fact that in his comedies – e.g. *Marriage, Italian Style* and *Yesterday, Today and Tomorrow*, both starring Loren and Mastroanni – de Sica would aim for a broad, generously Italian style without paying too much attention to details, there was the drawback of his none too fluent command of English. He was therefore reduced to mimicking what he wanted from the actors (perhaps a throwback to his neo-realist days when he worked exclusively with non-professionals), a method that Sellers naturally found both embarrassing and insulting. After just three weeks of shooting, he plotted to have de Sica replaced. When the movie's producer, John Bryan, suggested that a new director at such a late stage was hardly calculated to ease matters, Sellers tried to have *him* fired. In the end, the film was completed with everyone still on the payroll (and, a year later, Sellers consented to appear in yet another de Sica disaster, *Woman Times Seven*).

Though on this occasion his unethical antics might be considered justified, a disturbing pattern was beginning to emerge which would be repeated in movie after movie. He had a peculiar gift for alienating those who were trying most to help him. And what might once have been willingly excused as a regrettable side-effect of his ruthless pursuit of perfection had increasingly come to seem no more than the eruptions of an inflamed ego. He trampled on the feelings of others like some existential Inspector Clouseau. Sellers was a visibly unhappy man – unhappy with his work, unhappy with his marriage (whose apparently idyllic outer aspect was also the result of a dual 'performance' on his and Britt's part) and unhappy with himself. In the past, he had always managed to escape from the latter two by adopting another identity, but his current dissatisfaction with his work was subjecting that particular form of escape to rapidly diminishing returns. Slowly, the man of a thousand faces was coming face to face with himself.

5 P. S.
Your Show
Is Slipping

AN UNFUNNY thing happened to Peter Sellers on the way to success: he became a playboy. Which would be significant only to gossip columnists, except for the catastrophic effect this change had, not only on his performances but on his whole approach to movie teamwork. During the next few years, until *The Return* (or comeback) *of the Pink Panther* in 1974, he was to star in an almost unbroken sequence of flops, critically, commercially and, saddest of all (but by no means an automatic corollary of the other two categories), artistically. Even the later Panther films, enormously successful from a money-making point of view, were defeated game, set and match by the flair and invention of the original. Fans who in the past would have hated themselves for missing any of his appearances, who treated a new Sellers movie as an *event*, were now staying away from them in droves. At the same time, his own inexcusably boorish behavior on the set was to alienate even those who would once have claimed to be, on a more personal level, unconditional admirers of the man. The period that stretched roughly from *Dr. Strangelove* in 1964 to *Being There* in 1979, one year before his death, was for Sellers an artistic wasteland, rendered all the more poignant by the fact that in the latter movie, directed by Hal Ashby, he proved that his genius had not, as everyone supposed, deserted him. It had 'merely' gone into hibernation – over a long, cold winter of *our* discontent that lasted sixteen years.

What happened? Nothing, really, that could not have been anticipated in the character of Peter Sellers, the leading mimic of British cinema, or Peter Sellers, Goon, or even Peter Sellers, up-and-coming variety comedian. But to paraphrase Acton's celebrated dictum on power: Success corrupts, and absolute success corrupts absolutely. (There are, needless to say, numerous exceptions, but Sellers unfortunately was not among them.) The signs are too glaringly obvious to be ignored.

For example: Sellers' father died of a heart attack, while he himself survived *eight*. Such strikingly good fortune can affect its subject in one of two ways: he can be assailed by intimations of mortality, by a realization of just how slender is the thread attaching us to life; or he can see himself suddenly as one of the elect, clearly chosen by means of an almost miraculous revival to fulfil some outstanding destiny. Normally, one might suppose that the person would be caught midway between these two poles. Sellers, on returning to England after his heart attack, admitted to a firing squad of reporters at London Airport: "I will now have to alter my whole way of life. If I don't there won't be a Peter Sellers around much longer." Yet just a few days later he purchased his *83rd* automobile – a Ferrari 330, capable of speeds up to 150mph. When, during the shooting of *The Bobo* in 1967, he received word in Rome that Peg had just suffered a massive coronary at the Royal Northern Hospital in Holloway, he astonished everyone, Britt included, by choosing to stay on and complete the movie. He was his mother's son and if he had survived a heart attack, so then would she. A week later, she died. Sellers was beside himself at the idea that he had not been beside her.

His marriage also began to take on some rather curious overtones. Though, with carefully adjusted 'carefree' smiles, they were often to be seen in the company of such other front page couples as the Antony Armstrong-Joneses and Burton and Taylor, their relationship was in reality no more secure than those of their illustrious fellow socialites. Sellers was neurotically jealous, accusing Britt of adultery with Yul Brynner, her co-star in Franklin Shaffner's *The Double Man*, almost before she had even met him. And again during *The Bobo*, in which she appeared opposite him, he frequently threatened to have her replaced, making it embarrassingly evident to everyone that her presence in the film was entirely due to the fact that she had married him. Since, contractually, he reserved for himself the final say on the feminine lead, he certainly knew what he was talking about. But his sadistic on-off-on treatment of her casting (in her autobiography she confesses to having finally employed a little emotional blackmail to bluster her way into the role) was typical of his disposition at this period.

Before *The Bobo* there was *Casino Royale*, inspired by the first (and arguably the best) of Ian Fleming's James Bond novels. There, however, the inspiration ended. As the movie emerged, it boasted remarkably little in the way of coherent plotting, a fault that was compensated for by the numerous plots and counterplots hatched before and during its turbulent shooting. To begin with, it was financed, not by the producers of the regular Bond series, Harry Saltzman and Albert 'Cubby' Broccoli, but by

Charles Feldman of *What's New, Pussycat?* Having been acquired separately, the property proved to be something of a white elephant. Since Feldman could not use Sean Connery, he decided that the only possible solution was to send up the Bond persona, making *Casino Royale* a kind of farcical satire with only a very marginal connection to the original novel.

So the movie (whose cast, besides Sellers, included David Niven, Ursula Andress, Orson Welles, Joanna Pettet, Daliah Lavi, Deborah Kerr, Woody Allen, William Holden, Charles Boyer, John Huston, Barbara Bouchet, George Raft, Jean-Paul Belmondo, Peter O'Toole and the racing driver Stirling Moss) was a confused concoction in which, SMERSH having become all-powerful, the secret services of Britain, America, France and the Soviet Union combine to see how it can be foiled. They decide to persuade James (now Sir James) Bond out of retirement – by blowing up his country house. In the explosion 'M' is killed, and Bond travels to Scotland to console his widow and family, the McTarrys. But, unknown to him, they have been replaced by some agents from SMERSH and – oh forget it! Suffice to say that, at the climax of this incomprehensible farrago (for which, apart from the three writers credited, responsibility must also be borne by Billy Wilder, Ben Hecht, Terry Southern and Joseph Heller), *everyone* more or less turns out to be James Bond.

It was visibly intended to be a 'fun movie' *à la Pussycat*, except that on this occasion not even the cast gave a convincing impression of enjoying themselves. Which undoubtedly was the case. Joseph McGrath was originally hired as sole director, a risky choice for a multimillion dollar production as it was his very first feature. But he was a personal friend of Sellers who, over Feldman's better judgment, decided on him as the man most qualified to steer such a vast, leaky vessel (which already bore a striking resemblance to the Titanic) safely into port. McGrath, however, could not have realized that he would also have to deal with a severe and genuinely founded crisis that centered around Sellers' vanity. The crux of the movie (and, for once, of the original novel too) is a marathon game of baccarat played at Le Touquet between the evil genius behind SMERSH, Le Chiffre (Welles), and Bond – or rather, in the movie version, one of Bond's many surrogate figures, Evelyn Tremble (Sellers). But the latter, after a humiliating encounter with the gargantuan American actor-director, became obsessed with the notion that he was going to be upstaged – that, like some neurotic chess-master, his playing would suffer from the hostile vibrations of his charismatic co-star. He categorically refused to play the scene in Welles's presence. I.e. he insisted that McGrath film first Welles then, in a reverse angle, a reaction shot of himself, and so on.

All of which was perfectly feasible, especially as they would be sitting opposite each other across a baccarat table. But, apart from the fact that the lack of any establishing shot of the two players together would be unnecessarily disorienting for the spectator, actors tend to benefit greatly from a form of mutual feedback, even (or perhaps especially) if their personal relations are less than amicable. Sellers, whose work had already been blunted by a string of yes-men directors, was now prepared to deny himself the indispensable opportunity of playing opposite another actor. And his performance in *Casino Royale* is significantly one of the most featureless and lackluster of his entire career.

For that someone would have to be blamed. Sellers did not indulge in an excess of heart-searching: McGrath it was who had to go. And so he departed, concurrently with a press release to the effect that such an inexperienced filmmaker had never been intended to complete the movie, segments of which would now be allotted to different well-known directors. In the end, McGrath was credited jointly with John Huston, Ken Hughes, Val Guest and Robert Parrish. The Pink Panther had struck again.

If no amount of cooks could have spoiled a broth that was already rancid, it's equally true that they could scarcely improve matters. The movie was a fiasco, and rarely have so many and varied negative superlatives been brought to bear on a single production. Curiously, its producer, Feldman, died soon after in Hollywood.

But *The Bobo*, which followed *Casino Royale*, did not even possess the virtue of being spectacularly disastrous. Sellers had initially planned to direct it himself, but after his unhappy experience with *Mr. Topaze* he wisely decided that such a division of his attention would make it impossible for him to control his own performance. So he contented himself with directing the nominal director, the unfortunate Robert Parrish. There was an extremely unpleasant scene after shooting had finished when he suddenly announced to a flabbergasted Parrish that they were to share the directorial credit. (In fact, Parrish's name figures in conspicuous solitude and, given the result, Sellers could congratulate himself on a narrow escape.)

To put it as charitably as possible, *The Bobo* was ghastly. The plot – in order to launch a new career as Spain's first singing matador, a failed bullfighter must first seduce a local *belle* – was a (literally) cock-and-bull story, the performances uniformly bad and the direction perfunctory to the point of non-existence. Though Sellers was *hysterically* unfunny, even worse were his attempts to inject a touch of Chaplinesque pathos into the role and which made one's toes curl with embarrassment. The movie, wretchedly received by critics and public alike, was speedily consigned to an oblivion from which it should never have been dredged up in the first place.

In that same year, as if to add insult to injury, Sellers made a brief cameo appearance in another all-star farrago perpetrated by de Sica, the sketch movie *Woman Times Seven*. This time, it was not he but Shirley Mac-Laine who played seven roles – without succeeding in creating one real

character among them. She was supported by Lex Barker, Vittorio Gassmann, Elsa Martinelli, Robert Morley, Anita Ekberg, Alan Arkin and Michael Caine.

Trouble was brewing for Sellers himself and Woman Times Two. Britt and he could hardly bear to spend time in each other's company, as their marital life was increasingly beset by violent squabbling and sometimes physical aggression. He would accuse her of delusions of stardom, taunting her with being no more than Mrs. Peter Sellers, while she would accuse him of being . . . just Peter Sellers. On one occasion at London's Royal Garden Hotel she swallowed a half-dozen sleeping pills, not enough to kill herself with but more than enough to frighten him, In reparation, he offered her a new Italian sports car – their once passionate romance was rapidly turning into Alfa-Romeo and Juliet.

A rather more publicized affair at the time was with Princess Margaret, though whether the word 'affair' should be understood in a strictly carnal

sense is a matter still open to speculation. Undoubtedly, he was smitten with PM (as she was coyly nicknamed by her little set) and no love was lost between him and Roddy Llewellyn when the latter appeared to have usurped her affections. But friends who observed them together could never quite believe in the sexual side of their friendship. Sellers was someone who made Margaret laugh, a court jester who was often though not always allowed the jester's traditional privilege of speaking out with

unaccustomed licence. (It was rumored, too, that, having been awarded a CBE in 1965, he was now angling for the British actor's Oscar of Oscars, a knighthood.) Two jests with which the royal family (Margaret included) were 'not amused', however, were his smutty recording, *Fool Britannia*, and an embarrassing visit to the theater in their company to see *Son of Oblomov*, devised by and starring Spike Milligan. What offended the royal party was that Milligan suddenly interrupted the course of the play to indulge in some corny music hall cross-talk with Sellers. A specimen of their improvised humor: Milligan: "Why does Prince Philip wear red, white and blue braces?" Sellers: "I don't know. Why *does* Prince Philip wear red, white and blue braces?" Milligan: "To keep his trousers up!" Collapse of royal party.

Sellers' second marriage came to an abrupt end at the Excelsior Hotel in Rome, following a failed attempt at a final reconciliation on board his yacht (ominously named the 'Bobo') while cruising along Yugoslavia's Dalmatian coastline. They had cut short the trip to fly up to Rome, where just about everything went wrong. Sellers sulked on the plane, sulked in the hotel, sulked in the restaurant where they dined that evening and, on their return to the hotel, finally exploded – "gesticulating like a militant union leader", as Britt quaintly phrased it in her autobiography. At 3.30 that morning, he threw her out of the Excelsior and out of his life. In June 1968 they formally separated. Two months later divorce proceedings were underway and by December he was once more a bachelor.

He was now also a tax exile in Beverly Hills, with a Belgravia mansion as a useful *pied-à-terre* for those few weeks a year when he was permitted to reside in England. Hollywood offered him little, however, but cordial detestation. That *Evening Standard* interview continued to rankle and had undoubtedly caused him to lose the Oscar for which he was nominated in recognition of his triple performance in *Dr. Strangelove*. Nevertheless, he and Blake Edwards managed to resolve their artistic differences long enough to collaborate on *The Party*, the story of an Indian extra in Hollywood who is invited to an exclusive party when the producer of the movie which he has wrecked, intending to enter his name on a blacklist, inadvertently inscribes it on his guest list. Thereafter, the film records a series of disasters gravitating around the presence of this accident-prone Hindu, culminating in a scene with an elephant in the swimming pool and the house virtually disappearing beneath mounds of detergent suds.

Sounds unappealing? Yet the movie, while by no means a total success and fatally undecided as to whether it ought to be ambitious or unpretentious, proved to be one of the more likeable made by Sellers (and Edwards, for that matter) during this phase of their respective careers. To counteract the impression of *déja vu* (or *entendu*) created by his overfamiliar Indian accent, mannerisms and catch-phrases – "Birdie Num-Nums!" – there was, as usual with Edwards, a strong element of slapstick

te. P.S. as the bugler
npending flop 'Son of
Din' – *The Party*

p too many for the
ng Indian guest – *The*
968).

comedy that provided the springboard for some of the most elaborate sight gags in recent years. For example, the opening sequence when Sellers hilariously sabotages the movie *Son of Gunga Din*; his desperate attempts to dry out a Chagall painting (retrieved from the toilet bowl) which result in its being transformed into a smeary abstract one; and his mortifying pursuit of a recalcitrant shoe from lily pond to laden tray of hors d'oeuvres. Oddly enough, a few of the funniest ideas derived from other actors, in particular Steve Franken as a progressively drunk waiter whom we glimpse at one point, from the tantalizing vantage point of a swing door, being cold-bloodedly strangled by one of his sober colleagues.

But that visual *trouvaille* exemplified the dilemma of the movie as a whole. What Edwards was presumably aiming for was a comedy of situation, of a multiplicity of situations, in which the existence of any clear narrative line would take second place to what in most other comedies would be mere digressions. He was prepared to allow central events to take place almost offscreen, to relegate his most brilliant gags to a corner of the frame and to distribute the situation's humorous possibilities 'democratically' among the whole cast. Sellers' presence, therefore, could only be disruptive. He was a star, and had to be treated as such. Amusing as he is, one has the distinct impression that he is performing in quite another movie.

In *I Love You, Alice B. Toklas*, he played, not Gertrude Stein but Harold Fine, obsessed not with 'a rose is a rose is a rose' but with '60s flower power. An asthmatic Los Angeles lawyer about to be married, he becomes involved through a complicated series of misunderstandings with a beautiful but brainless flower-child (Leigh Taylor-Young) and on the eve of his wedding defects to hippiedom himself. Though the movie (directed by Hy Averback and co-scripted by the director-to-be Paul Mazursky) began promisingly with some mild but occasionally telling satire of an affluent, matriarchal Jewish community (Sellers staking out with surprising conviction territory that would be definitively claimed by Woody Allen), it left no stoned hippie unturned in its cliché-ridden depiction of Southern California's 'alternative lifestyles.' (The cute use of Alice B.'s name in the title refers not, of course, to her friendship with expatriate literati but to her notorious recipe for marijuana brownies.) Like too many of Sellers' movies, it came and went without anyone paying very much attention to its passage. To this day Mazursky, originally intended to direct it, refuses to speak about his experience with its star.

Times were hard. Sellers, who had once been able to command almost a million dollars for a movie (on *Dr. Strangelove*, Kubrick had only been half joking when he sourly remarked that he had secured three performances for the price of six), was now offering himself for less than a tenth of that fee (plus a percentage of the profits – hardly a compensation, in view of the dismal success rate of his recent efforts). He was prepared to accept assignments – in publicity, for example – that astonished friends not intimate enough to realize how financially vulnerable he was beginning to feel. But when Gillette, the razor manufacturers, invited him to contribute to a campaign for a new product by listing a few people and objects he considered to epitomize the word 'style', he agreed without demanding a fee. (Another participant was Noël Coward, who might have figured on everyone else's list.) As his choice (like that spoken by Woody Allen into a tape-recorder at the end of *Manhattan*) offers some autobiographical clues, it's worth taking a closer look at it:

My wife   A red Lamborghini Miura   El Cordobes
Private Eye Magazine   Habit Rouge de Guerlain
Leicaflex and Summicron-R f/2 50mm, Elmarit-R f/2.8 35mm & 90mm
The music of Antonio Carlos Jobim   A Baglietto 18m motor yacht
The Daily Mirror   Hi-Fi   Vodka   Shakespeare
Sid Perelman   Roast beef and Yorkshire pudding
Italian shoes   Some Chinese food   Fred

Here, pell-mell, are to be found Sellers the fanatic of gadgets (with a fetishistic, almost James Bond-like attention to minutiae), Sellers the expensively groomed (French perfume and Italian shoes) behind whose sleek surface can still be detected his earlier self's lower-middle-class insecurity (Yorkshire pud. and the ubiquitous Fred), Sellers the connoisseur of verbal extravagance equally at home with humdrum tabloid journalese (Perelman and *The Daily Mirror*). No less noteworthy, but by default, is the omission of any great painter or composer, giving one the impression that Sellers had never read anything resembling literature (the inclusion of Shakespeare seems little more than 'token' and scarcely constitutes a *choice*) nor had ever glanced at any landscape or architecture. It's the list of someone too busy jetting around the world to take a long, leisurely look at himself, the list of a playboy to whom 'art' was something you had stereophonically piped into your Belgravia *pied à terre* or Bel Air mansion while relaxing in the jacuzzi.

In some respects, it paints a fairly accurate picture of both his life and his aspirations. After a brief liaison with Mia Farrow, he became involved with Miranda Quarry, daughter of a former Conservative cabinet minister, Lord Mancroft. Their long, often stormy affair ended rather surprisingly in marriage at Caxton Hall registry office in August 1970, Miranda's 'bridesmaids' being two of her Pekinese dogs. As Sellers succinctly put it to journalist David Lewin: "She was my intellectual superior and I met people through her who were in a different social class. It was difficult." Which reminds one of a remark made by Britt to another journalist (she was speaking of the Englishman in general rather than Peter Sellers in particular, but all the same. . .): "He is frightened of women who are as bright as he is. They challenge his masculinity and make him insecure." Though every one of his four wives was as young and beautiful as

Off on honeymoon to M
Carlo with bride numbe
three Miranda Quarry (

Miranda, marriage this time around seemed little more than a formality. One might say that from the beginning it didn't last.

Meanwhile, he was ploughing on with his professional career, making one error of judgment after another. Terry Southern's novel *The Magic Christian* was a drily humorous satire on human rapacity, as reflected in the distorting mirror of the grandiose hoaxes perpetrated by its zillionaire hero, Guy Grand, who is prepared to fritter away a fortune if it will prove to what humiliating lengths the world will go in its pursuit of the green stuff. For a movie version to work at all, it would logically have to be as offensive as Grand's own schemes, and only a director as ruthless as Kubrick, say, could have pulled it off and still made money for his producer. In any case, Joseph McGrath (he who was so summarily dealt out of *Casino Royale*) would scarcely have been anyone's first choice for such a daunting task. Yet, despite the fiasco of their previous collaboration and its bitter aftermath, it was McGrath whom Sellers, producing the film for his own newly formed company, finally settled on.

Dispiritingly but not unexpectedly, when *The Magic Christian* emerged on the screen, it bore a greater resemblance to the chaotic *Casino Royale* than to Southern's terse little squib. An all-star cast – Ringo Starr, who had already lent his ineffable presence to *Candy*, that travesty of another Southern novel, Richard Attenborough, Laurence Harvey, Christopher Lee, Raquel Welch, Wilfrid Hyde White and those two Monty Pythonites, John Cleese and Graham Chapman (also credited with 'additional material' to the screenplay) – succeeded in removing the original's sting by turning its narrative into a series of woefully unfunny vaudeville acts. Harvey performed a coy striptease on stage while reciting Hamlet's 'To be or not to be' soliloquy, Milligan played a traffic warden forced to chew up and swallow his own ticket, etc. As Guy (now Sir Guy) Grand, Sellers contributed a familiar sketch of aristocratic eccentricity, but tended to be swamped by the glut of guest stars. And the transposition of the plot to an English setting – with Grand setting his malicious sights on such tame, hackneyed sacred cows as Sotheby's, the Oxford-Cambridge Boat Race and Crufts' Dog Show – removed all sense of authenticity from a work that had been very much in tune with the anti-Establishment currents of the '60s. From the evidence of an interview which he gave to *Esquire*, Sellers genuinely believed he was making a subversive, muckraking, anti-authoritarian movie; it was greeted, however, like a breath of stale air.

Following it was *Hoffman*, directed by Alvin Rakoff and adapted from his own novel by Ernest Gebler. Sellers played a lonely middle aged businessman obsessed with his pretty young secretary (Sinead Cusack). Though encumbered with a tediously obtrusive subplot involving the criminal activities of the typist's brother, it amusingly charted Hoffman's manically single-minded pursuit of a victim whose reluctance gradually shifts into compliance. In theme, and in the refreshing modesty of its ambitions, the film was oddly reminiscent of Sellers' earlier British comedies, *The Battle of the Sexes* or *The Dock Brief*, and would certainly have been a more fully achieved work if only it had been made then. The actor was now a middle-aged man himself, which rather took the edge off his impersonation of middle age. There were also too many moonstruck interludes when the characters were allowed simply to revel in each other's company – strolling over the heath, playing piano together – without the director offering much to hold the spectator's attention. Nevertheless, for starved Sellers-watchers, *Hoffman* did offer a few crumbs, table scraps from the banquets of only a few years back. In particular, there was a characteristic little vignette which demonstrated – as *The Battle of the Sexes* had done in the scene where the old accountant tries to murder his tormentor while pretending to seduce her – that his forte was less for multiple impersonations than for catching the frenzy of an ordinary man obliged to disguise his intentions and whose mask will keep slipping at the least propitious moments.

This sequence, as in the earlier movie, takes place in a kitchen. Hoffman has lured the young stenographer to his apartment, where he is determined to present her with a seamless façade of smooth worldliness. But behind the scenes – or rather, behind the service hatch separating kitchen from living room – things are very different. Though busy rifling through cupboards with feverish impatience, each time he passes in front of that open hatch window he abruptly turns into a model of suave self-control, belied only by a resounding crash offscreen a few moments later. A modest, not unlikable little film, it failed totally at the box-office . . . precisely because, in an era of all-or-nothing blockbusters, it was just a modest, not unlikable little film.

And, with *The Magic Christian*, it appeared to signal a temporary return to England from Hollywood, which lasted (with one unfortunate exception) until his triumphant comeback as Inspector Clouseau. He would later confess to journalist Clive Hirschhorn: "It is great getting away from London every now and then, but it's greater coming back. Los Angeles and all that sunshine certainly have their charms, but this is my home. And you know what they say about there being no place like it." Yes, we do, but it's not impossible that his consistent lack of success across the Atlantic (both *Lolita* and *Dr. Strangelove* were shot in England) contributed in some way to this enthusiasm for a national cinema that was already all but moribund.

Suddenly, he was very much in view – in an odd variety of roles. He would accompany Princess Margaret to Ronnie Scott's jazz club in Soho, where the saxophonist Scott one evening read out a piece of dubious verse composed for the occasion by Spike Milligan (in his best McGonagall manner): "Wherever you are, wherever you be, please take your hand off the Princess's knee." Sellers' subsequent 'no comment' – ("There's only one thing I can say to Spike about Princess Margaret and myself: 'We are just good friends.' You mustn't read anything else into this") – was exactly the kind of ambiguously phrased denial that was calculated to rekindle old rumors. On a very different occasion, he made a peace tour of Belfast in the fall of 1971 with the yoga cult leader Swami Vishnu Devananor, showering 10,000 antiwar leaflets over the city from a private aircraft and later autographing many of them for the finders. He also presented a large bouquet of flowers to a Mrs. Irene Gallagher, whose baby daughter Angela had been killed by a sniper's bullet. He became the godfather of his old friend Graham Stark's daughter in a ceremony at the 'actor's church', St. Paul's in Covent Garden. And he appeared more frequently on television, most notably as the White Rabbit in Jonathan Miller's controversial adaptation of *Alice's Adventures in Wonderland*, switching to the March Hare for William Sterling's dreary, unmagical film version in 1972.

In 1970 he was signed for *There's a Girl in my Soup*, based on Terence Frisby's long-running stage farce about a lecherous TV personality whose macho sense of superiority is challenged and eventually outmaneuvered by a cheerfully amoral dumb blonde. It was to be produced by John Boulting, directed by his brother Roy and financed by Columbia, who envisaged it as a terrific vehicle for a young comedienne on the verge of stardom, Goldie Hawn. The Boultings had an uphill task persuading Columbia's board of directors that only Sellers could play the role, just as during the shooting they had to use all their powers of persuasion with members of the crew alienated by Sellers' tantrums. In one sense they were right, as the movie made money for everyone concerned; in another, however, they could not have been more mistaken. *There's a Girl in my Soup* is a disaster for several reasons, the most glaringly obvious of which is the casting of Sellers.

Basically, the role called for a Cary Grant, but any competent actor with a light touch would have been preferable to a mimic, however brilliant. Frisby's play, set exclusively in the hero's bachelor apartment (which the movie version 'opens out' in very half-hearted fashion), was a hyper-conventional romantic comedy of a type that is as current now as it was then. And precisely what its well-worn but still effective conventions

required was a duo of romantic leads, male and female. Goldie Hawn, though a poor man's Monroe or a Judy half-Holliday, satisfied this demand with a familiar but funny portrayal of arch, dewy-eyed sexual knowingness. Sellers, on the other hand, misguidedly opted to play the male lead as if it were a character role, as if it were Captain Bligh or his own Fred Kite. Throughout the film one felt the presence of the actor ticking away behind the character, and so noisily that it all but drowned out whatever natural charm the 'real' Peter Sellers might have brought to the role. He winked, he leered, he smirked – to either minimal or distressing effect. Where a less talented but more disciplined comedian might have managed to prop up the flimsy structure erected by Frisby, Sellers brought it crashing down about him. The movie's box-office success only proved that a million satisfied customers could be, and on this occasion were, wrong.

Vanity through the look glass for "Robert Danve *There's a Girl in my Sou* (1970).

6 The Pink Panther Strikes Again... And Again

I F SELLERS' standing in the movie community was boosted by the success of *There's a Girl in my Soup*, the respite was a fleeting one. In fact, his career entered its most dispiriting phase of all, during which one movie would be shelved before completion, another never released, a third released, as it were, on parole. Rarely has any top international star fallen so low in mid-career, with such headlong speed. Though he would confess to friends his determination to become more selective in his choice of roles, it seemed as if some inner compass which was already malfunctioning had gone completely askew. So much so that his mind actually turned to the much-hated theater again, though without any positive result. Already in 1969, he had planned to star in a play by Jane Arden, *The Illusionist*, which he termed "the most important stage work of the year". To be produced by Jack Gold at London's Round House theater, it was finally cancelled owing to his film commitments (and to the fact that his leading lady, Sheila Allen, broke her leg during rehearsals). Then in December 1971, at the official opening of the St. George's Theatre in Southwark, he announced his intention to "do some Shakespeare" in the near future. For years vague rumors had circulated that he would play Richard III for the National Theatre – though, as he would possibly find himself unconsciously impersonating Olivier's quasi-definitive performance, it was doubtless all for the best that it came to nothing.

His next movie, *A Day at the Beach* (directed by one Simon Hesera), remains a total mystery. Shot in Denmark, with Sellers reputedly playing a homosexual character, it hasn't been seen since. He himself never referred to it again. Another of the 'commitments' which prevented him from appearing in Jane Arden or Shakespeare was a comedy rather unfortunately entitled *Where Does It Hurt?*, which he made in Hollywood under the 'direction' of Rod Amateau, the poor man's Hy Averback. For those who hurt 'only when they laugh' this inept farce was the perfect cure. Sellers played – in his by now almost customary suave manner – an unscrupulous medic whose scheming is foiled by his voluptuous nurse/ mistress (Jo Ann Pflug, a name that is funnier than anything in the movie). It was colorless, tasteless and, with its crude gags on malpractice and appendectomies, decidedly malodorous.

But each of his appearances appeared to have reached a kind of nadir – until the next one came along. (This is, of course, when viewed from hindsight. At the time, Peter Sellers had long since ceased to be a name to conjure with, and those movies which did surface were seen by almost as few spectators as the others that didn't). The vicious circle that was governing his career – one bad performance leading to an even less attractive offer – had begun to spiral out of control. Sellers described to a journalist the slight difference he had noted in the kind of treatment he received at the hands of the Hollywood moguls. "The first time I went I was feted like King Feisal. I remember I'd just done five smash hits in a row and I could do no wrong. The red carpet was rolled out from the airport to the Bel Air Hotel and I just couldn't get over it all. My most recent film there was the comedy *Where Does It Hurt?*, in which I played an American doctor. I think I saw the mid-way and the end of the star system in Hollywood." Which is one way of putting it. . .

In 1972 he was approached by a young director, Clive Rees, about to make his first feature, *The Blockhouse*, based on a novel by Jean-Paul Clébert. The novel in turn had been inspired by the authentic story of some prisoners of war (of various nationalities) who sought refuge in a German-built blockhouse during the first wave of air attacks on D-Day 1944. Bombing caused the main entrance to cave in; but, fortified by a plentiful supply of food, wine and candles, they settled down to a mole-like existence in its underground halls and corridors. When it was excavated in 1951, two of the group were still alive, having lived out at least four years in total darkness. One died within minutes, the other within days, of being rescued. (In view of this, and the fact that apparently none of them kept a diary, it's difficult to know just how closely the film's narrative substance sticks to fact and how much is based on mere speculation.)

Not a light comedy, obviously. Apart from the introductory sequence detailing the attack (Rees apparently had only one aircraft at his disposal but deployed it so cunningly that one never questioned his lack of means), the movie's sole decor was the dark blockhouse itself. Which meant that almost every image, illuminated solely by candles, was framed around a tiny pool of light into which the actors (Sellers apart, these included Charles Aznavour, Per Oscarsson, Peter Vaughan and Jeremy Kemp) would occasionally drift. Added to which, the quality of the sound recording (at least, in the print screened at the National Film Theatre in January 1981) was abominable, so that one neither saw nor heard enough to feel capable of judging anyone's performance. Rees did not even reward the patience of his audience with a climactic burst of sunlight and fresh air, ending the film on a totally black screen as the candles finally ran out. He declared: "It's a film about human beings. Too many directors are able to hide behind fight scenes, glamor and explosions. *The Blockhouse* did not offer us anything like that." No indeed; yet there was something deeply perverse, even self-destructive, in so denying the medium its potential for the play of light and shade, in entombing the camera along with the unfortunate actors for a full ninety minutes. Unsurprisingly, the movie was all *longueurs*.

Sellers played Bouquet, a gentle, retiring schoolmaster who preserves his sanity by scrawling poetry on the walls as if it were a kind of intellectual graffiti. As to whether his performance was, in the words of the film's producer Antony Rufus Isaacs, "the best thing he's ever done . . . his Macbeth", it's impossible to say, given the somber impenetrability of both sound and image. *The Blockhouse* was screened at the 1973 Berlin Festival, then consigned to some Wardour Street vault, a fate not unlike that of its protagonists (except that they were buried *alive*).

Before beginning his next movie, another marginal and offbeat British production, he turned up with Spike Milligan, Harry Secombe, musicians Max Geldray, Ray Ellington and various members of the original Goon orchestra in BBC radio's *The Last Goon Show of All*, broadcast as part of the Corporation's Jubilee celebrations in 1972 (though Milligan typically referred to it as being for the fiftieth anniversary of Director-General Lord Hill's legs – "they've been together now for fifty years"). The event was much publicized and Prince Charles, one of the Goons' most ardent fans, greatly regretted that naval duties prevented him from being able to attend in person. Aside from its own high entertainment value, the show could only have heightened the nostalgia of those fewer and fewer admirers who ached to see Sellers return to the kind of surreal humor with which he had made his name.

Certainly, they would have been disappointed by Anthony Simmons' *The Optimists of Nine Elms* (sometimes known simply as *The Optimists*). Based on one of the director's own short stories, the movie recounted the edgy friendship which two slum children strike up with an eccentric, rather senile old busker, Sam, and his mongrel dog. The extent of their parents' ambition is to move into one of the clean but drably impersonal council flats on the Nine Elms estate, but old Sam, with his poignant line in corny music hall patter (" 'Appens to all of us." "What?" "Being born.") fleetingly offers them a vision of a freer existence, one un-

The Goons reassemble[part of the BBC's 50th anniversary celebratio[(April, 1972).

trammeled by material necessities, that is as tempting as it is deceptive. Though its brand of sharply etched realism (the terrifying squalor of the estate, the relentless working class routine) would seem to run counter to Sellers' larger than life screen presence, he gave one of his more affecting performances, undoubtedly calling on his own unsentimental memories of fifth-rate vaudeville performers in his portrayal of Sam. He looked, moreover, disturbingly old and frail, with a gauntness that could not be wholly attributed to make-up. But as a commercial venture the movie was doomed by its reluctance ever to raise its voice. Though the critics were kinder than usual, it did not receive wide distribution.

Apparently unfazed by its lack of success, he tried to obtain funding for another movie set in London's East End, an adaptation of a play by Bernard Kops, *By the Waters of Whitechapel*, about a middle-aged Jew unable to make the psychological break from his mother. As a subject, of course, it had a certain personal relevance for Sellers, who appeared to remain tied to his mother's apron strings even beyond the grave. He had regular 'chats' with her via some of his favorite mediums, generally old ladies living in musty Kensington flats and endlessly poring over Tarot cards. Wherever he was domiciled, a little shrine would be erected to her memory and a candle lit faithfully every Friday. His relationship with Peg and the past that she represented was intensified in proportion as the names of acquaintances were peremptorily shifted from his address book to what he called his 'shit-list'. Several of those demoted, however, were Miranda's friends rather than his own. The powerful attraction he had once felt for the poised, moneyed, titled milieu in which she moved had long since cooled, especially as, with the aid of a private detective, he was beginning to discover that she had been unfaithful to him.

It was at this lowest ebb of his life that he would threaten to commit suicide or even take religious vows and enter a monastery. As unstable as ever – he once knocked a doctor friend unconscious for rashly suggesting that many of his ailments were self-induced – he was no longer enjoying a sufficient degree of success, with all the attendant adulation, for most people to be able to forgive such bad behavior. Unable to 'run away from home', so to speak, he would run away and take his home with him. For example, seeking a tax haven and no longer caring to live in Southern California, he bought a huge estate in an Irish village on the outskirts of Dublin. There he installed a young American secretary, who for most of the time found herself deserted by her employer as he rushed off to film in Hollywood or London. Finally, she packed her bags and returned to Los Angeles. Shortly after, Sellers sold up and himself took up residence in England again.

In 1973 he was offered six roles in succession – all of them, however, in just one movie, the latest Boulting Brothers comedy, *Soft Beds, Hard Battles*. This was about a brothel in Occupied Paris and the rambling, episodic adventures of its inmates and Madam (a painfully miscast Lila Kedrova) to foil both the Nazi and Japanese secret services simultaneously. Sellers was seen as a doddery French general, a thin-lipped Gestapo agent, an aristocratic Japanese officer, the usual chinless English major, the President of France and Adolf Hitler – then added the brief cameo of a radio newscaster to make it a round baker's half-dozen. The anxieties plaguing him while he was filming *Dr. Strangelove* that such multiple role-playing was little more than a gimmick seem not to have applied to this movie, where a gimmick was indeed all it turned out to be.

He was intermittently amusing, and the extraordinary range of his characterizations was startling in itself; less admirable was the fact that his mimicry was patently no longer rooted in observation. 'Prince Kyoto' proved indistinguishable from any number of crude Oriental impersonations, down to the usual breathy cackle of an accent. His Gestapo henchman, replete with belted trench-coat and granny glasses, hardly differed from the same thing badly done in some straight B movie. The peculiar spark that separated his talent from that of numerous other character comedians – from Benny Hill, say – had from the evidence of his recent

Four military types for the price of one – *Soft Beds, Hard Battles* (1973).

work been temporarily snuffed out. Needless to say, *Soft Beds, Hard Battles* passed almost unnoticed through England's dwindling number of cinemas.

It was during its shooting, however, that he encountered Liza Minnelli. They met at an intimate dinner party. The following evening she invited herself and a crowd of fellow performers from her London Palladium show to his diminutive Belgravia mews flat. And little more than twenty-four hours later, they were announcing their engagement to an astonished world. Sellers, it should be remembered, was still a married man, even if separated from Miranda in every sense except the strict legal one. Their affair was what is usually called a 'whirlwind' one, and lasted almost exactly a month. According to Bert Mortimer, the fundamental drawback was Liza's highpowered life style. "Liza, alas, was definitely too much for Peter to handle. He was working all day filming the appropriately named *Soft Beds, Hard Battles*. Liza was out every night at the Palladium and when her show was over she wanted excitement. The result was that a shattered Sellers would slump into the make-up chair

the next morning and fall fast asleep. The poor make-up artist was frequently driven to distraction by Peter's snorts, snores and head turnings." His head had certainly been turned but, though one of his more celebrated affairs, it also proved to be one of the briefest and he soon returned to Christina 'Titi' Wachtmeister, the daughter of the Swedish ambassador to Washington.

She was subsequently to join him in Cyprus, where he began filming *Ghost in the Noonday Sun* under the direction of Peter Medak. Never heard of it? In fact, it has remained the ghost of a movie, as it was never completed and so never released. An anarchic pirate farce starring Sellers as a wily, double-dealing ship's cook, Spike Milligan (who co-scripted it), Antony Franciosa and Peter Boyle, it was headed for trouble virtually from the very first day. Sellers' monstrous egotism was the eye (or 'I') of several concurrent hurricanes. He took an instant dislike to Franciosa and, receiving a very minor scratch to his eye in their big dueling scene together, immediately flew off to England to consult his opthalmologist (that it had been cured was confirmed by his return to Cyprus in the company of the exquisite 'Titi'); he abandoned the shooting on another occasion to attend Princess Anne's wedding; he attempted to have the producers fired and he had Medak replaced, catastrophically, by Milligan, thereby totally forfeiting what little credulity he could still command from among the rest of the cast. The horrified backers, Columbia (already bitten with *Casino Royale*), eventually managed to back out, using as their excuse a ten-day sea storm that blew up in Cyprus on the last days of shooting. The company repaired to England ostensibly to film the final sequence on its meteorologically more reliable south coast the following spring, and the production was quietly shelved.

So too – or so it appeared – was Sellers' career. Surely this time he was finished, having been virtually blacklisted (like the timid little Indian of *The Party*) by everyone who counted in Hollywood. Bitterly conscious of having ruined both his public and private life, he was close to a nervous breakdown. But, like the Pink Panther's, his own 'return' and 'revenge' were at hand. Though Sellers had made three highly profitable comedies with director Blake Edwards, their collaboration ended with both vowing never to work with the other again. Edwards, however, had also been suffering a lean period, particularly with the duo of movies starring his wife, Julie Andrews (*Darling Lili*, one of the costliest flops in Hollywood history, and *The Tamarind Seed*). He began – almost simultaneously with Sellers, it would appear – to cast his mind back on that naggingly memorable panther (now the star of his own TV show) and that stumblebum of the Sureté who had bumbled his way into a fortune for both director and star. In the interim period between *A Shot in the Dark* and the first of the new sequels, *The Return of the Pink Panther*, a half-hearted attempt had been made to revive the formula in a movie baldly titled *Inspector Clouseau*. It had not, however, been directed by

"Sam" with his two friends – The Optimists of Nine Elms

Edwards (but by Bud Yorkin) or starred Sellers (but Alan Arkin). Though briskly inventive in its own right, and though Arkin subtly fleshed out the central character, making his pratfalls more gracefully deadpan, Clouseau *was* Peter Sellers. The movie didn't 'take'.

So in 1974, after Sellers had made a brief appearance as Queen Victoria in Joseph McGrath's *The Great McGonagall*, a deal was signed. *The Return of the Pink Panther* co-starred Christopher Plummer as the Phantom (David Niven's role), Catherine Schell as the vapidly winsome romantic interest and, of course, Herbert Lom as the eternally long-suffering Chief Inspector Dreyfus. It was practically a family reunion: the familiar theme music by Henry Mancini, a supporting cast that included David Lodge and Graham Stark, and delicious animated credit-titles by Richard Williams (in which the Panther imitates, Sellers-style, such movie icons as Carmen Miranda, George Raft, Groucho Marx, Fred Astaire, Chaplin, Mickey Mouse and Frankenstein's monster). A permanent addition to the series was Burt Kwouk as Cato, Clouseau's houseboy, apparently hired for the sole purpose of leaping out at his master from the unlikeliest hiding-places in order to keep his self-defense reflexes in trim.

No one was amused. "Victoria" with the Sco（Spike Milligan） – The McGonagall (1974).

The plot complications, involving a false Phantom who stings the genuine one into retaliation, are too convoluted to enter into here, especially as they represented only a series of pegs on which to hang a number of comic set-pieces. Best for first, perhaps, with Clouseau, demoted to the lowly rank of patrolman, berating a blind beggar while just behind him a bank is being robbed; he even retrieves part of the loot dropped by the gang and politely passes it through the window of their getaway car. And

seau'' in 'immaculate'
se amuses Catherine
— *The Return of the*
anther (1974).

r, houseboy "Cato"
wouk) takes it in the
om his master.

'Have you got a licence
your minké?' – The Ret
the Pink Panther (1974

much of the film's most effective humor is pure cartoon. When Clouseau, learnedly examining the heavy metal arm with which a diamond robbery has been effected, lets it fall hard on his crotch, his voice correspondingly soars to a shrill falsetto. When he turns a radio switch, it's as cautiously as if he were discovering the combination to a safe. When telephoned by Dreyfus with the introductory snarl "This is the man who would like to see you dead and buried!", Clouseau thoughtfully inquires, "Are you the head waiter from the little bistro. . . ?" But one's fears that the original concept of the character had begun to coarsen were depressingly confirmed by the excessive number of hackneyed slapstick props – a vacuum cleaner run riot, a revolving door, a cigarette lighter in the form of a revolver, a soda siphon and a swimming pool into which Clouseau *twice* drives his car – and by the increasingly tedious repetition of Dreyfus's decline into twitching, gibbering madness (the climax of the movie finds him in a padded cell scrawling 'Kill Clouseau' on the wall with a pen grasped between his toes).

This would appear to be a minority opinion, however. It was a colossal box-office success and, with those which followed, turned Sellers the

The unmist
''Clouseau'

"Chief Inspector Dreyfu[
fires a cigarette lighter a[
hated colleague – The P[
Panther Strikes Again ([

has-been almost overnight into one of the world's highest paid performers. Before embarking on *The Pink Panther Strikes Again*, he made an
appearance in *Murder By Death*, Neil Simon's broad but diverting spoof
on classic literary and cinematic detectives (directed by Robert Moore).
He played Sidney Wang, whose gnomically meaningless fortune cookie
epigrams and 'Number One Son' suggested a not too distant cousin of
Charlie Chan. Others involved in this amiable farrago were Elsa Lanchester as Jessica Marbles (Agatha Christie's 'Miss Marple'), Peter Falk as Sam
Diamond (Dashiell Hammett's 'Sam Spade') and David Niven and Maggie Smith as Dick and Dora Charleston (Hammett's 'Nick and Nora
Charles' of *The Thin Man*, another title that got attached to its sequels
long after the original character had disappeared). Bringing up the rear
were Alec Guinness, teamed with Sellers for the first time since *The
Ladykillers*, as the blind butler Bensonmum ("Not Benson, mum," he
corrects Maggie Smith, "Bensonmum.") and the novelist Truman

...who? – *The Pink*
...r Strikes Again (1976).

Capote, bearing a strange resemblance to Sellers' own Quilty in *Lolita*. Sellers himself brought a welcome hint of Goonish *chinoiserie* to his role and obviously enjoyed himself hugely.

In *The Pink Panther Strikes Again* there is a scene in which, while Clouseau stalks around his apartment in a characteristic martial arts stance awaiting a surprise attack from Cato, Dreyfus in the flat beneath, plotting revenge on his tormentor, is in the process of boring a spyhole through the ceiling. After Cato's pounce finally materializes, he and his master demolish a vast four-poster bed, causing plaster, rubble and water to pour down on the unfortunate Dreyfus. End of gag, one would suppose. But no – by a series of slapstick contrivances, it actually ends a few moments later with Clouseau encased in an inflatable hunchback costume (which naturally inflates) wafted over the rooftops of Paris toward the gargoyle-infested steeples of Notre-Dame. And the comic overkill of this undisciplined multiplication of gags was symptomatic of the way the whole movie, like its immediate successor *The Revenge of the Pink Panther* (a *Godfather* send-up), had taken off into a kind of grotesquerie closer to the Three Stooges than the Goons. Sellers' disguises were now

"Clouseau's" suspect
remains unruffled – Th
Panther Strikes Again (

less a matter of infallibly precise accents than of outrageous wigs and false noses: Clouseau as a Robert Newton-like old sea-dog with a wobbly stuffed parrot perched on his shoulder, Clouseau as a snowy-haired Einstein lookalike whose make up progressively melts until strips of false flesh hang from his face like marzipan stalactites, Clouseau as Toulouse-Lautrec, a frequent choice of third-rate mimics. In *The Pink Panther Strikes Again*, Dreyfus's demented frustration at the success of his incompetent underling transforms him into a comic-strip villain, holding the world to ransom with his Doomsday Machine (another melancholic reminder of how far Sellers had declined since the turning point of *Dr. Strangelove*).

Whether in spite or because of the way the character had been vulgarized, these movies figured along with the parodies of Mel Brooks and other practitioners of the belly laugh (e.g. *The Kentucky Fried Movie*) on *Variety*'s listings of the most successful comedies in Hollywood's history. So successful that yet another reached the planning stage: *The Romance of the Pink Panther*, to be directed either by Sidney Poitier, a rather odd choice, or Sellers himself, an even odder one. To persuade him

Disguised as a color
*The Revenge of the P
Panther* (1978).

104

"Clouseau" dons the ga[...]
Mafia chief – *The Rever[...]
the Pink Panther (1978[...]

to don Clouseau's trenchcoat once more, United Artists had come up with a mind-boggling contract. He would receive no less than three million dollars up front plus 10 per cent of the gross. Which meant that if *The Romance* turned out to be the box-office bonanza of the others, his total income from it would amount to around eight million dollars. As it happened, however, the future was to take a different direction, and *The Revenge* proved to be the Panther's swan song.

Meanwhile . . . in 1974 Miranda finally sued for divorce, 'Titi' having been replaced in Sellers' affections by an attractive young companion named Lorraine McKenzie. Sellers had a new, outwardly more mature attitude toward women, expressed in an interview he gave to Clive Hirschhorn: "The real bliss I get out of life now comes directly from the meditation I do. There's no doubt about that. No woman has been able to give me that sense of inner peace and tranquillity. On the contrary, women – and I know what I'm talking about – often cause pain and anguish. Yoga does just the opposite. But," he added, "I still enjoy women, and I need them around. You can be hooked on yoga *and* women at the same time, you know."

His life at this juncture was governed by yoga almost as much as by astrology. He had been introduced to Oriental discipline by the Indian musician and friend of the Beatles, Ravi Shankar: "Yoga appeals to me because it is completely free of dogma but embraces all religions. I should know. I have been tutored in them all." His new, spacious apartment in London's seedy Victoria district, directly beneath that of the Laurence Oliviers, was furnished in '60s Katmandu style, complete with candles, the faint but pungent odor of incense, and walls and carpets in soothing saffron and brown. Astrology, of course, had always been one of his preoccupations, with charts drawn up not only for himself but for his three children.

As with his first wife, it was Dennis Selinger, old pal and sometime agent, who introduced him to his last, Lynne Frederick, at a party given at his home. She was 21, almost thirty years his junior, an English beauty who had acted mostly on television. After they had lived together for a year, he proposed to her on the very day she was about to accept a film assignment in Russia whose shooting schedule had been fixed at five months. She said yes to the proposal and no to the offer of work. In view of Lynne's quiet, unsophisticated nature, her unshowbizzy taste in clothes, her cooking talents which ran to such humble, 'Fred'-like dishes as shepherd's pie and Yorkshire pudding, a host of friends and journalists predicted wishfully that this time the marriage just might work. Sellers had already demonstrated the depth of his feelings for Lynne by his refusal to attend the Royal Charity Première of *The Pink Panther Strikes Again*, in the presence of Prince Charles, because the equerry in charge of protocol judged Peter Sellers' 'girlfriend' an unsuitable person to be included in the presentation line-up after the screening. The Prince, gracefully enough under the circumstances, found the movie 'hilarious'.

As it happened, the movie also had a troubled opening in Paris. René Goscinny, creator of the French cartoon strip *Astérix*, had sent Sellers a manuscript entitled *The Master of the World* concerning an evil scientific genius who from his sinister castle threatens the earth with extinction. It was shortly after returned to him with a brief rejection note. When he saw *The Pink Panther Strikes Again*, however, Goscinny immediately telephoned his lawyer to have all copies seized, charging Sellers and Blake Edwards with having plagiarized his script. The problem was eventually smoothed over and the movie enjoyed a normal release throughout the country.

Despite the generally indulgent treatment of Sellers' latest marriage by

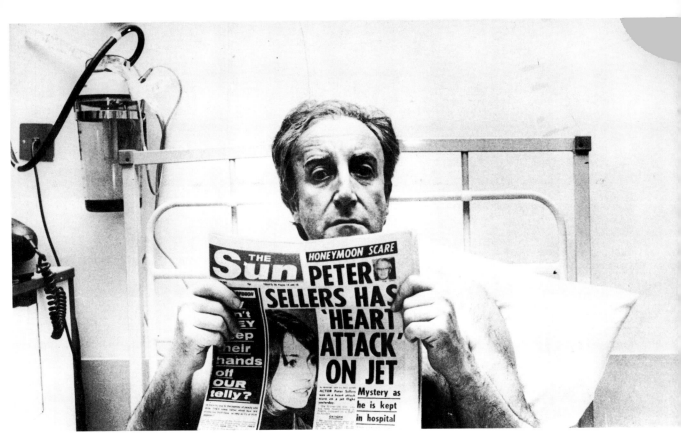

the press, one person was adamantly convinced that it would not last: Lynne's mother, Irene Frederick, an English television executive (her father, divorced, was American). "What mother can be expected to approve the marriage of her daughter to such a man," she moaned to the press, "My heart bled for her. To me their marriage was doomed from the start." Not until her son-in-law's death, in fact, did she ever write to Lynne or get in touch with her. And though her forebodings proved not entirely unjustified, she had made a bad tactical error in airing her grievances in such classic mother-in-law style. Her outburst, coupled with Sellers' own professional comeback and the fact that his temperament appeared to be mellowing, caused the bitchy gossiping about him in both the English and American press to ease up. Especially as in 1976, flying back to London from the South of France, Sellers suffered a serious malaise, 'publicly' diagnosed as food poisoning, the result of having eaten oysters in Nice. In reality, it had been a minor heart attack; and at the Charing Cross Hospital he had a small pacemaker fitted into his body. He referred to himself jocularly as a "partly bionic man" and insisted that, with the exception of jogging, there was no physical activity too strenuous for him.

Though two of the most intriguing projects of his whole career were in the offing – *The Alien* (no relation to the smash hit of the same name), a science-fiction movie in which he was to play an Indian again but this time for the most celebrated of Indian directors, Satyajit Ray, and *Being There* from the short novel by Jerzy Kosinski – he turned next to a film

"Chauncey Gardner" i natural habitat – *Being* (1980).

Another happy couple;
with Lynne Frederick.

which had all the earmarks of his recent poor judgment. It was a comic
version of the rusty old Ruritanian romance by Anthony Hope, *The
Prisoner of Zenda*. The signs were not encouraging. Firstly, it was to be
directed by Richard Quine, with whom Sellers had already worked (and
squabbled) on the ill-fated *Bobo*. And he intended the leading feminine
role, that of Princess Flavia, to be taken by his wife, a tactic which also
called up disturbing memories of the earlier movie and Britt Ekland's
participation. He himself would tackle, as was the tradition with this
story, two roles: Prince Rudolph, the effete heir to the throne of Ruritania,
and his double who replaces him, on this occasion Sidney Frewin, a
hansom cabbie with a thick cockney accent. Sellers also appeared briefly
in the movie's opening sequence as the old King, a pioneer aviator, who
breathes his last simultaneously with his punctured balloon.

As to whether a warhorse like *The Prisoner of Zenda* really benefits
from parody (Blake Edwards having already failed to send it up in his
farcical spectacular *The Great Race*), the question was never likely to be
answered by this leaden comedy. Though its visuals were occasionally
fetching (due to location work in Vienna), verbal felicities rarely rose
above the Prince's inability to pronounce the letter 'R' – his 'Dwat it!"
making him sound like a Mittel-European Elmer Fudd – and someone, of
course, remarking that he "has trouble with his R's". . . Or else Sellers
raising his eyebrow at the unintentionally ribald mispronounciation of
the word 'Count' . . . Lynne was cute but made little impression.

e Rudolph'' or
ey Frewin''; P.S.
two roles – *The*
er of Zenda (1979).

Sellers had been on better behavior than usual during the shooting though as always, when struggling into the skin of a new character, withdrawn and testy, notably with his wife. But real trouble started when the producer, Walter Mirisch, screened the movie for him privately before its gala première. Halfway during the screening Sellers became visibly restive and began to utter mild obscenities under his breath; and when it was over, he rose, screamed "You'll be hearing from me!" and stormed out. Next morning Mirisch received an icy 13-point memo from his star, outlining his various grouses. Later Sellers explained to a reporter: "I don't know how I held myself in check that evening. The version I saw was so bad. It could have been a really lovely adventure story in the classic tradition – with a new twist. And it still could: the material is all there. But Mirisch has tried to turn it into a sort of poor man's *Pink Panther* and shot extra scenes using doubles which I knew absolutely nothing about. The result is a disaster." When the film opened (to

The 168-year-old "Fu Manchu" – *The Fiendi*
of Dr. Fu Manchu (198(

extremely brutal reviews) he appeared to be less critical, perhaps to avoid compromising Lynne's career; but, though his description of it as a disaster was fair enough, it's hard to see how any more inspired version could have emerged from such limp material.

His plan to work with Satyajit Ray having fallen through, Sellers put all his energy into setting up the movie of *Being There*. He had been captivated by Kosinski's brilliant fable of a nonentity who rises to the White House like a bubble, transparent and always about to burst, and had an unshakable conviction that only one actor could do justice to the serenely passionless Chance: himself. Chance, he felt, might well be his last chance. So he set about convincing Kosinski, and Hal Ashby (*Harold and Maude*, *Coming Home*), who was slated to direct it.

The unique challenge posed by the role of Chance the Gardener (alias Chauncey Gardner) was that of impersonating someone *who simply wasn't there*. In Kosinski's novel, the character is never fleshed out by verbal descriptions of age and physique. Chance has no past. No identity. Most dramatically for Sellers, no accent. Totally illiterate and ignorant of

112

the ways of the world, he has lived most of his life contentedly tending the garden of his mysterious benefactor, known simply as the Old Man. And in this Edenic garden, there has been neither snake nor Tree of Knowledge – the ubiquitous television, to which he is addicted, serves only to multiply the areas of his ignorance. Chance has been, as the black maid Louise succinctly puts it, "shortchanged by the Lord", both mentally and, it is hinted, physically. Sellers, resolved to recover the glittering, sharp-edged precision of his earlier work after so much coarse-grained clowning, was denied the very foundation of the mimic's art: the possibility of honing a type down into a living, breathing individual.

It wouldn't be an exaggeration to affirm that his marriage almost foundered on his desperate search for some characteristics that he could attach to this man without a character. While filming in Ashville, North Carolina, he was almost unapproachable and had so completely withdrawn into the cocoon of his character that it began to frighten Lynne. Once he had hit on the voice – a softly understated version of Stan Laurel's American-inflected North Country accent – the rest clicked infallibly into place: the staid overcoat and Homburg hat, the dated but well-cut suits slightly too short in the trouser-leg and, especially, the hypnotically placid expression from which every trace of emotion had been rigorously expunged. Without question, the performance was one of the greatest of his career. It won him the American National Board of Review award of 'Best Actor' of the year and a second Oscar nomination. After years of approaching type-casting with the popular but limited Clouseau, he demonstrated that his genius was still intact and could be tapped if both director and role were strong enough. He demonstrated too that, though chronically incapable of playing 'himself' (*The Mouse That Roared*, *There's A Girl In My Soup*), he had the power to give flesh to 'no one'.

In this, of course, he was much aided by both Ashby (who with *Being There* made what is by far his best movie) and Kosinski (whose adaptation of his 150-page squib actually improves on the original). If the film version failed to make the romantic interludes between Chance and the Washington socialite, Eve Rand (played by Shirley MacLaine), convincing, it worked perfectly when charting Chance's leisurely but irresistible (in both sense of the word) ascension to the Presidency. Wonderfully off-center gags abounded: Chance, accustomed to having his meals served him by Louise, accosting a harassed black housewife in the street and plaintively enquiring about his lunch; or, endearingly, watching his own appearance on a TV talk show and, as has always been his custom, almost immediately switching channels. Much of the movie's sly, subtle humor derived from the spectator's uncertainty as to whether what he was seeing or hearing was actually intended to be funny. The joke was often on us; and such familiar devices of deadpan comedy as the double-take and the slow burn were more frequently to be seen on the faces of the

"Fu Manchu's" advers. Scotland Yard detectiv "Nayland Smith" – *The Fiendish Plot of Dr. Fu Manchu* (1980).

audience. Chance, gazing around him in an escalator, pensively remarks, "This is a *very* small room"; he greets the President of the United States (a marvellous study in restrained drollery from veteran Jack Warden) with the unanswerable comment, "You look much smaller on TV"; and, asked by Eve if he is related to Basil and Perdita Gardner, he answers solemnly, "No, Eve, I'm not related to Basil and Perdita." In view of the character's inability to do more than repeat, either his own few words or those which have just been addressed to him, Sellers must have been allotted the smallest vocabulary of any major role in the history of the sound film.

Any biographer of Peter Sellers has to resist the temptation to end right there. What followed in the last months of his life was basically a matter of reruns: speeded-up repeats of his marital problems, his dubious professional judgment, his egocentric behavior and, of course, his heart attack. But life does not resemble the perfect biography and rarely ends as tidily as one might wish. Nevertheless, between the completion of *Being There* and his final, fatal heart attack the following year, Sellers was – visibly – dying. When he flew to Paris to make his last film, *The Fiendish*

Plot of Dr. Fu Manchu, he startled the cast with his emaciated, sickly appearance. He had lost too much weight too quickly and his skin had begun to crinkle slightly, like parchment. For years his doctors had warned him of the need to rest, but always ahead loomed the specter of uncompleted business. Like a compulsive gambler, he had to keep playing till luck came his way again. With *Being There* it had. And since he had completed it, since he was a rich, none too healthy man in his late middle-age and since *Fu Manchu* (like *The Prisoner of Zenda*, a spoof of a popular 'classic') was patently not the kind of movie that would add an inch to his reputation, one can only conjecture that, as happened with almost all his 'roles', he had finally been swallowed up by his own public persona – Peter Sellers, jet-setting comic genius, temperamental husband, controversial superstar. If so, he played it out with a vengeance.

Lynne's first inkling that the rift in their marriage might lead to eventual divorce came when a friend read her over the telephone a newspaper interview in which Sellers had announced to the world that they were finished. She was shattered. Though they were virtually living apart – she in Los Angeles and he either on his Mediterranean yacht or in a new villa which he had bought in Gstaad – the cruel, arrogant way the decision had been taken by him alone, and in public, hurt her profoundly. To columnist Roderick Mann she admitted: "It's an awful way to hear about the end of your marriage. Now we have both consulted lawyers, though nothing's happened yet. We talk every day and I know he feels just as badly as I do about the break-up. Peter says he thought it would be forever. But so did I." During the filming of *Fu Manchu*, however, he telephoned her incessantly, alternately sending her long-stemmed roses or telegrams ambiguously signed "Your nearly ex-husband". Later, to everyone's astonishment, she joined him in Paris. (After Sellers' death, and with the revelation of the will, Lynne would categorically deny that there had ever been talk of a divorce.)

Meanwhile 'creative differences' had already removed Richard Quine from the new project, another potential director John G. Avildson had gone the same way even prior to the completion of the script, and when filming finally got under way the director was a young Englishman, Piers Haggard. Every weekend Sellers would fly to his Swiss villa; one Monday morning he didn't return. Doctors, troubled by his persistent physical fatigue, had advised complete rest for a month in a Geneva clinic. The film was postponed until the early spring of 1980. At which point it was Haggard (who had doubtless earned his name in the interim) whom Sellers decided had to be replaced, taking over direction himself. Suffering hours of agony as Fu Manchu's make up was applied then exerting himself on both sides of the camera (and further adding to his problems by playing both the evil old Chinaman and his arch-enemy, Nayland Smith), Sellers gave the impression of committing suicide in a peculiarly slow and disagreeable fashion.

The Fiendish Plot of Dr. Fu Manchu, premièred after his death, was received by the critics either mercilessly or regretfully, as if they felt he ought not to have survived long enough to make it. To be sure, one could find a certain poignancy in the central plot conceit (while his cut-throat minions attempt to extract a powerful 'elixir vitae' from a stolen gem, the aged Fu is shudderingly kept alive by a series of increasingly violent electric shocks). And in the welter of adverse criticism, Sellers' touching, finely detailed performance as Smith – an Englishman of the old school in flannel trousers, houndstooth check jacket and woollen tie – passed sadly unnoticed. There was, too, an occasional amusing exchange – Fu, on being apprised of some new disaster befalling his organization: "That is good news." "Why is it good news, Master?" "Because I'm in no position to receive bad news." Or Goonish echo – in order to kidnap Queen Mary at a Botanical Garden, Fu's followers disguise themselves as "Englishmen and flowers". But the script and supporting performances lacked discipline, direction had suffered irrevocably from Sellers' tampering and, when the movie ended with a rejuvenated Fu parodying Elvis Presley for no earthly reason save that of having as spectacular a climax as possible, it was painfully obvious that it had run out of both steam and ideas.

Wan, exhausted, his body disturbingly shrunken, Sellers prepared to deliver his own *coup de grâce*. After collapsing in Dublin, he flew to Cannes where *Being There* was being screened in the Festival competition. Then off to Hollywood. Then back to London for a long-standing reunion date with Milligan and Secombe. And it was in London, at the Dorchester Hotel, that he suffered a severe coronary on July 22. Lynne flew over from the States, and Britt arrived at the Middlesex Hospital in company with her daughter Victoria. Two days later, with his son Michael at his bedside, Peter Sellers died of 'natural causes'.

The funeral at Golders Green crematorium was private, the mourners filing out of the chapel to Glenn Miller's 'In the Mood', music chosen by Sellers himself. A few weeks later, on September 9 (his birthday), a memorial service was held at St. Martin-in-the-Fields church just off Trafalgar Square. The presiding cleric, Canon John Hester, vicar of Brighton and a lifelong friend, greeted the starry congregation with "Welcome to this birthday party for Peter Sellers". Lynne arrived alone; Anne with her two children, Michael and Sarah; Britt was absent. The Goons were there, of course, along with Lord Olivier, Lord Snowdon, Michael Caine, scriptwriter Denis Norden, Graham Stark, David Lodge and the ever resilient Cato, Burt Kwouk. David Niven, his neighbor at Gstaad, gave an address that was whimsically affectionate without ever minimising the actor's difficult character. The rest of the congregation comprised almost a thousand people who had never known Sellers personally but considered themselves close friends of Bluebottle, Bloodnok, Fred Kite, Clouseau and Chance the Gardener.

Afterword

THE CONTROVERSY surrounding Peter Sellers while he lived didn't die with him. His will having been altered six months before his death, it was revealed that he had bequeathed almost the entire estate – a conservatively estimated four million pounds – to Lynne. The three children (who had already been provided for by their father with trust funds of twenty thousand pounds) were left the bizarre and insulting sum of 750 pounds apiece, to which was appended some fatherly advice: "It's time you stood on your own feet." The children immediately protested, instructing their lawyers to have the probate frozen. Said the eldest, Michael: "We feel Dad has humiliated us by this will, which he obviously drew up on the spur of the moment in one of his black moods. He was always changing his will. He used it as an instrument of blackmail on all members of the family. At the time we must have been out of favor. If Dad had lived another six months and proceeded with his divorce from Lynne, the entire estate would have rightfully passed to the three of us. Lynne is lucky. She was cut out of an earlier will."

Lynne's answer was curt and left no doubt as to her ultimate intentions. "The will is what Peter wanted and people should have enough respect for him to honor his wishes. If it had gone the other way, I wouldn't have dreamed of contesting it." The family split was complete when just six months after Sellers' death Lynne married the well-known television personality, David Frost, in Teberton, a picturesque village in Suffolk. Sellers' daughter Sarah commented sourly: "We are still mourning his loss."

But perhaps it would be more appropriate to end by quoting a brief letter sent to the London Evening Standard by the broadcaster Joy Nichols, who had taken exception to the facetious tone of David Niven's memorial address:

"When my twins Richard and Victoria were born 18 years ago in Mt. Sinai Hospital, New York City, a six-foot high basket of flowers arrived from London with the message: "Clever girl. Love, Peter Sellers."

My stock was high. All the nurses came to visit the lady who knew Peter Sellers. It didn't surprise me. The flowers, I mean.

Peter was also a sweetie."

In later years.

Filmography

PENNY POINTS TO PARADISE   1951
GB Advance Films   77 mins black & white
Director Tony Young
Cast Harry Secombe, Alfred Marks, Paddy O'Neil, Peter Sellers, Vicky Page

DOWN AMONG THE Z MEN   1952
GB E.J. Fancey Prod   71 mins black & white
Director Maclean Rogers   *Producer* E.J. Fancey
Screenplay Jim Grafton and Francis Charles   *Photography* Geoffrey Faithfull
                                    Music Jack Jordan
Cast The Goons (Peter Sellers, Harry Secombe, Spike Milligan, Michael Bentine), Carole Carr

ORDERS ARE ORDERS   1954
GB Group Three/British Lion   78 mins black & white
Director David Paltenghi   *Producer* Donald Taylor
Screenplay Donald Taylor, Geoffrey Orme (play by   *Photography* Arthur Grant
   Ian Hay and Tony Armstrong)   *Music* Stanley Black
Cast Peter Sellers, Brian Reece, Margot Grahame, Raymond Huntley, Tony Hancock

JOHN AND JULIE
1955

GB Group Three   82 mins Eastmancolor

Director William Fairchild   *Producer* Herbert Mason
Screenplay William Fairchild   *Photography* Arthur Grant
                                       Music Philip Green

Cast Colin Gibson, Leslie Dudley, Peter Sellers, Moira Lister, Wilfred Hyde White, Sidney James, Andrew Cruickshank

LADYKILLERS
1955

GB Ealing Studios   90 mins Technicolor

Director Alexander Mackendrick   *Producer* Michael Balcon
Screenplay William Rose   *Photography* Otto Heller
                                       Music Tristram Cary

Cast Alec Guinness, Cecil Parker, Herbert Lom, Peter Sellers, Katie Johnson, Frankie Howerd, Danny Green

CASE OF THE MUKKINESE BATTLE HORN
1955

GB Cinead Ltd   29 mins black & white

Director Joseph Sterling
Cast Peter Sellers, Spike Milligan, Dick Emery

THE SMALLEST SHOW ON EARTH (US – Big Time Operators)
1957

GB British Lion/Launder & Gilliat   81 mins black & white

Director Basil Dearden   *Producer* Michael Relph
Screenplay William Rose and John Eldridge   *Photography* Douglas Slocombe
                                       Music William Alwyn

Cast Bill Travers, Virginia McKenna, Margaret Rutherford, Bernard Miles, Peter Sellers, Leslie Phillips, Francis de Wolff

THE NAKED TRUTH (US – Your Past Is Showing)
1957

GB Rank   92 mins black & white

Director Mario Zampi   *Producer* Mario Zampi
Screenplay Michael Pertwee   *Photography* Stan Pavey
                                       Music Stanley Black

Cast Peter Sellers, Terry Thomas, Peggy Mount, Dennis Price, Shirley Eaton, Georgina Cookson

TOM THUMB
1958

GB MGM/Galaxy   98 mins Eastmancolor

Director George Pal   *Producer* George Pal
Screenplay Ladislas Fodor   *Photography* Georges Périnal
                                       Music Douglas Gamley and Kenneth Jones

Cast Russ Tamblyn, Jessie Matthews, Peter Sellers, Terry-Thomas, Alan Young, June Thornburn, Ian Wallace

UP THE CREEK
1958

GB Byron Film Prod | 83 mins Hammerscope/black & white

Director Val Guest | *Producer* Henry Halsted
Screenplay Val Guest | *Photography* Arthur Grant

Cast David Tomlinson, Peter Sellers, Wilfred Hyde-White, Vera Day, Tom Gill, Michael Goodliffe, Lionel Jeffries, Reginald Beckwith

CARLTON-BROWNE OF THE F.O. (US – Man In A Cocked Hat)
1958

GB Charter Films/British Lion | 87 mins black & white

Director Roy Boulting and Jeff Dell | *Producer* John Boulting
Screenplay Jeff Dell and Roy Boulting | *Photography* Max Greene
| *Music* John Addison

Cast Peter Sellers, Terry-Thomas, Ian Bannen, John Le Mesurier, Raymond Huntley, Luciana Paoluzzi

THE MOUSE THAT ROARED
1959

GB Columbia/Open Road | 85 mins Technicolor

Director Jack Arnold | *Producer* Carl Foreman
Screenplay Roger MacDougall and Stanley Mann (novel by Leonard Wibberley) | *Photography* John Wilcox
| *Music* Edwin Astley

Cast Peter Sellers (playing 3 parts), Jean Seberg, Leo McKern, David Kossoff, William Hartnell, MacDonald Parke, Harold Kasket.

I'M ALL RIGHT, JACK
1959

GB British Lion/Charter | 104 mins black and white

Director John Boulting | *Producer* Roy Boulting
Screenplay: Frank Harvey and John Boulting (novel: Private Life by Alan Hackney) | *Photography* Max Greene
| *Music* Ken Hare

Cast Peter Sellers, Ian Carmichael, Irene Handl, Richard Attenborough, Terry-Thomas, Dennis Price, Liz Frazer, John Le Mesurier, Margaret Rutherford, Sam Kydd

THE RUNNING, JUMPING, STANDING STILL FILM
1959

GB Peter Sellers Prod/British Lion | 11 mins black & white

Director Dick Lester | *Producer* Peter Sellers
Conceived by Peter Sellers (Dick Lester, Mike Fabrizzio and Spike Milligan)

Cast Peter Sellers, Spike Milligan

THE BATTLE OF THE SEXES
1960

GB Prometheus | 83 mins black & white

Director Charles Crichton | *Producer* Monja Danischewsky
Screenplay Monja Danischewsky (story: 'The Catbird Seat' by James Thurber) | *Photography* Freddie Francis
| *Music* Stanley Black

Cast Peter Sellers, Constance Cummings, Robert Morley, Jameson Clark, Moultrie Kelsall, Alex Mackenzie, Roddy McMillan, Donald Pleasance, Ernest Thesiger

TWO WAY STRETCH
1960

GB British Lion/Shepperton
87 mins black & white

Director Robert Day
Screenplay John Warren and Len Heath

Producer M. Smedley Aston
Photography Geoffrey Faithfull
Music Ken Jones

Cast Peter Sellers, Lionel Jeffries, Wilfred Hyde-White, Bernard Cribbins, David Lodge, Maurice Denham, Beryl Reid, Liz Frazer, Irene Handl, George Woodbridge

NEVER LET GO
1961

GB Rank/Julian Wintle – Leslie Parkin
91 mins black & white

Director John Guillermin
Screenplay Alun Falconer

Producer Peter De Sarigny
Photography Christopher Challis
Music John Barry

Cast Richard Todd, Peter Sellers, Elizabeth Sellers, Adam Faith, Carol White, Mervyn Johns, Noel Willman

THE MILLIONAIRESS
1961

GB 20th Century Fox
90 mins Cinemascope/De Luxe

Director Anthony Asquith
Screenplay Wolf Mankowitz (play by Bernard Shaw)

Producer Pierre Rouve
Photography Jack Hildyard
Music Georges Van Parys

Cast Peter Sellers, Sophia Loren, Alastair Sim, Dennis Price, Vittorio De Sica, Gary Raymond, Alfie Bass, Miriam Karlin, Noel Purcell

MR TOPAZE (US – I Like Money)
1961

GB Dimitri de Grunwald/MGM
84 mins Cinemascope/Color

Director Peter Sellers
Screenplay Pierre Rouve (based on a play by Marcel Pagnol)

Producer Pierre Rouve
Photography John Wilcox
Music Georges Van Parys

Cast Peter Sellers, Nadia Gray, Martita Hunt, Herbert Lom, Leo McKern, Billie Whitelaw, John Le Mesurier

THE ROAD TO HONG KONG
1961

GB Melnor Films
91 mins

Director Norman Panama
Screenplay Norman Panama

Producer Melvin Frank
Photography Jack Hilyard
Music Robert Farnon

Cast Bing Crosby, Bob Hope, Dorothy Lamour, Joan Collins, Robert Morley (Peter Sellers, David Niven, Frank Sinatra and Dean Martin)

ONLY TWO CAN PLAY
1962

GB British Lion/Vale
106 mins black & white

Director Sidney Gilliat
Screenplay Bryan Forbes (novel 'That Uncertain Feeling' by Kingsley Amis)

Producer Launder and Gilliat
Photography John Wilcox
Music Richard Rodney Bennett

Cast Peter Sellers, Mai Zetterrling, Virginia Maskell, Richard Attenborough, John Le Mesurier, Raymond Huntley, Kenneth Griffith

LOLITA
1962

GB MGM/Seven Arts/AA/Anya/Transworld
152 mins black & white

Director Stanley Kubrick
Screenplay Vladimir Nabokov (from his novel)

Producer James Harris
Photography Oswald Morris
Music Nelson Riddle

Cast James Mason, Shelley Winters, Peter Sellers, Sue Lyon

WALTZ OF THE TOREADORS
1962

GB Rank
105 mins Technicolor

Director John Guillermin
Screenplay Wolf Mankowitz (play by Jean
    Anouilh)

Producer Peter de Sarigny
Photography John Wilcox
Music Richard Addinsell

Cast Peter Sellers, Margaret Leighton, Dany Robin, John Fraser, Cyril Cusack, Prunella Scales

THE DOCK BRIEF (US – Trial and Error)
1963

GB MGM
88 mins black & white

Director James Hill
Screenplay John Mortimer and Pierre Rouve
    (play by John Mortimer)

Producer Dimitri de Grunwald
Photography Edward Scaife
Music Ron Grainer

Cast Peter Sellers, Richard Attenborough

HEAVENS ABOVE
1963

GB British Lion/Charter
118 mins black & white

Director John Boulting
Screenplay Frank Harvey and John Boulting

Producer Roy Boulting
Photography Max Greene
Music Richard Rodney Bennett

Cast Peter Sellers, Isabel Jeans, Cecil Parker, Brock Peters, Ian Carmichael, Irene Handl, Eric Sykes,
    Bernard Miles

THE WRONG ARM OF THE LAW
1963

GB Romulus
94 mins black & white

Director Cliff Owen
Screenplay John Warren and Len Heath

Producer Aubrey Baring, E.M. Smedley Aston
Photography Ernest Steward
Music Richard Rodney Bennett

Cast Peter Sellers, Lionel Jeffries, Bernard Cribbins, Dave Kaye, Nanette Newman, Bill Kerr,
    John Le Mesurier

THE PINK PANTHER
1963

USA United Artists
113 mins Technirama

Director Blake Edwards
Screenplay Maurice Richlin and Blake Edwards
Producer Martin Jurow

Photography Philip Lathrop
Music Henry Mancini
Animation De Patie-Freleng

Cast Peter Sellers, David Niven, Capucine, Claudia Cardinale, Robert Wagner, Brenda de Banzie,
    Colin Gordon, Burt Kwouk

DR. STRANGELOVE 1963

GB Columbia 93 mins black and white

Director Stanley Kubrick
Screenplay Stanley Kubrick, Terry Southern
  Peter George (novel: 'Red Alert' by Peter
  George)

Producer Victor Lyndon
Photography Gilbert Taylor
Music Laurie Johnson

Cast Peter Sellers, George C. Scott, Peter Bull, Sterling Hayden, Keenan Wynn, Slim Pickens,
  Tracy Reed, James Earl Jones

THE WORLD OF HENRY ORIENT 1963

USA United Artists 106 mins Panavision/De Luxe

Director George Roy Hill
Screenplay Nora and Nunnally Johnson (novel
  by Nora Johnson)

Producer Jerome Hellman
Photography Boris Kaufman, Arthur J. Ornitz
Music Elmer Bernstein

Cast Tippy Walker, Merri Spaeth, Peter Sellers, Angela Lansbury, Paula Prentiss, Phyllis Thaxter,
  Tom Bosley, Bibi Osterwald

A SHOT IN THE DARK 1964

USA United Artists 101 mins Panavision/De Luxe

Director Blake Edwards
Screenplay Blake Edwards and William Peter Blatty

Producer Blake Edwards
Photography Christopher Challis
Music Henry Mancini

Cast Peter Sellers, Elke Sommer, George Sanders, Herbert Lom, Tracy Reed, Graham Stark, Burt
  Kwouk

WHAT'S NEW PUSSYCAT 1965

USA/France United Artists 108 mins Technicolor

Director Clive Donner
Screenplay Woody Allen

Producer Charles K. Feldman
Photography Jean Badal
Music Burt Bacharach

Cast Peter Sellers, Peter O'Toole, Woody Allen, Ursula Andress, Romy Schneider, Capucine,
  Paula Prentiss

THE WRONG BOX 1966

GB Columbia 110 mins Technicolor

Director Bryan Forbes
Screenplay Larry Gelbart and Burt Shevelove
  (novel by Robert Louis Stevenson, Lloyd
  Osbourne)

Producer Bryan Forbes
Photography Gerry Turpin
Music John Barry

Cast Ralph Richardson, John Mills, Michael Caine, Peter Cook, Peter Sellers, Dudley Moore,
  Wilfred Lawson, Nanette Newman, Tony Hancock, Thorley Walters, Irene Handl

AFTER THE FOX 1966

USA/Italy United Artists 103 mins Panavision/Technicolor

Director Vittorio de Sica
Screenplay Neil Simon and Cesare Zavattini

Producer John Bryan
Photography Leonida Barboni
Music Burt Bacharach

Cast Peter Sellers, Victor Mature, Britt Ekland, Lilia Brazzi, Paola Stoppa, Akim Tamiroff, Martin
  Balsam

CASINO ROYALE
1967

GB Columbia　　　　　　　　　　　130 mins Panavision/Technicolor

Directors John Huston, Ken Hughes, Val Guest, Robert Parrish, Joe McGrath, Richard Talmadge

Screenplay Wolf Mankowitz, John Law, Michael Sayers (novel by Ian Fleming)

Producer Charles Feldman, Jerry Bresler
Photography Jack Hildyard
Music Burt Bacharach

Cast David Niven, Deborah Kerr, Peter Sellers, Orson Welles, Ursula Andress, Woody Allen, William Holden, Charles Boyer, John Huston, George Raft, Dahlia Lavi

THE BOBO
1967

USA Warner Bros　　　　　　　　　　　105 mins Technicolor

Director Robert Parrish

Screenplay David R. Schwarz (novel: 'Olimpia' by Burt Cole)

Producer David R. Schwarz
Photography Gerry Turpin
Music Francis Lai

Cast Peter Sellers, Britt Ekland, Rossano Brazzi, Adolfo Celi, Hattie Jacques, Ferdy Mayne, Kenneth Griffith, John Wells

WOMAN TIMES SEVEN
1967

USA/France Embassy/20th Century Fox　　　　　　　　　99 mins Pathé Color

Director Vittorio de Sica

Screenplay Cesare Zavattini

Producer Arthur Cohn
Photography Christian Matras
Music Riz Ortolani

Cast Shirley Maclaine, Peter Sellers, Rossano Brazzi, Alan Arkin, Patrick Wymark, Michael Caine, Vittorio Gassman, Lex Barker

THE PARTY
1968

USA United Artists　　　　　　　　　98 mins Panavision/De Luxe

Director Blake Edwards

Screenplay Blake Edwards and Tom and Frank Waldman

Producer Blake Edwards
Photography Lucien Ballard
Music Henry Mancini

Cast Peter Sellers, Claudine Longet, Marge Champion, Fay McKenzie, Steven Franken, Buddy Lester

I LOVE YOU ALICE B. TOKLAS
1968

USA Warner/Seven Arts　　　　　　　　　93 mins Technicolor

Director Hy Averback

Screenplay Paul Mazursky and Larry Tucker

Producer Charles Maguire
Photography Philip Lathrop
Music Elmer Bernstein

Cast Peter Sellers, Jo Van Fleet, Joyce Van Patten, Leigh Taylor-Young, David Arkin, Herb Edelman

THE MAGIC CHRISTIAN
1969

GB Commonwealth United/Grand Films　　　　　　　95 mins Technicolor

Director Joseph McGrath

Screenplay Terry Southern, Joseph McGrath, Peter Sellers (novel by Terry Southern)

Producer Dennis O'Dell
Photography Geoffrey Unsworth
Music Ken Thorne

Cast Peter Sellers, Laurence Harvey, Ringo Starr, Richard Attenborough, Christopher Lee, Spike Milligan, Yul Brynner, Roman Polanski, Raquel Welch

HOFFMAN
1970

GB ABP/Longstone
113 mins Technicolor

Director Alvin Rakoff
Producer Ben Arbeid
Screenplay Ernest Gebler (from his novel and
play)
Photography Gerry Turpin
Music Ron Grainer

Cast Peter Sellers, Sinead Cusack, Jeremy Bulloch, Ruth Dunning

THERE'S A GIRL IN MY SOUP
1970

GB Columbia
96 mins Eastman Color

Director Roy Boulting
Producer John Boulting
Screenplay Terence Frisby (from his play)
Photography Harry Waxman
Music Mike D'Abo

Cast Peter Sellers, Goldie Hawn, Tony Britton, Nicky Henson, John Comer, Diana Dors, Judy
Campbell

WHERE DOES IT HURT?
1971

USA Josef Shaftel Prod.
88 mins Color

Director Rod Amateau
Producer Rod Amateau and William Schwarz
Screenplay Rod Amateau (from his and Budd
Robinson's novel 'The Operator')
Photography Brick Marquard
Music Keith Allison

Cast Peter Sellers, Jo Ann Pflug, Rick Lenz, Eve Druce

ALICE'S ADVENTURES IN WONDERLAND
1972

GB 20th Century Fox
101 mins Eastman Color/Todd-AO

Director William Sterling
Producer Derek Horne
Screenplay William Sterling (based on
Lewis Carroll)
Photography Geoffrey Unsworth
Music John Barry

Cast Fiona Fullerton, Michael Crawford, Robert Helpmann, Peter Sellers (March Hare), Dudley
Moore, Spike Milligan, Dennis Price, Flora Robson, Rodney Bewes, Ralph Richardson

THE BLOCKHOUSE
1973

GB Galactacus Prod/Audley Ass.
93 mins Eastman Color

Director Clive Rees
Producer Anthony Isaacs, Edgar Bronfman Jnr.
Screenplay John Gould, Clive Rees (Based on the
novel by Jean-Paul Clebert)
Photography Keith Goddard
Music Stanley Myers

Cast Peter Sellers, Charles Aznavour, Per Oscarsson, Peter Vaughn, Nicholas Jones

THE OPTIMISTS OF NINE ELMS
1973

GB Chettah/Sagittarius
110 mins Eastman Color

Director Anthony Simmons
Producer Adrian Gaye, Victor Lyndon
Screenplay Anthony Simmons (from his novel)
Photography Larry Pizer
Music George Martin

Cast Peter Sellers, Donna Mullane, John Chaffey, David Daker, Marjorie Yates

SOFT BEDS, HARD BATTLES
1973

GB Rank/Charter
107 mins Color

Director Roy Boulting
Producer John Boulting
Screenplay Roy Boulting and Leo Marks
Photography Gil Taylor
Music Neil Rhoden

Cast Peter Sellers, Lila Kedrova, Curt Jurgens, Gabriella Licudi, Jenny Hawley

GHOST IN THE NOONDAY SUN — 1973

GB Cavalcade/World Film Services — Color

Director Peter Medak
Screenplay Evan Jones and Spike Milligan

Producer Thomas Clyde, Ben Kadish
Photography Larry Pizer

Cast Peter Sellers, Spike Milligan, James Villiers, Peter Boyle, Antony Franciosa

THE GREAT McGONAGALL — 1974

GB Darlton — 89 mins Eastman Color

Director Joseph McGrath
Screenplay Joseph McGrath and Spike Milligan

Producer David Grant
Photography John Mackey
Music Derek Warne, John Shakespeare, Spike Milligan, Joseph McGrath

Cast Peter Sellers, Spike Milligan, Julia Foster, Julian Chagrin, John Bluthal, Valentine Dyall

THE RETURN OF THE PINK PANTHER — 1974

GB United Artists — 113 mins De Luxe

Director Blake Edwards
Screenplay Frank Waldman and Blake Edwards

Producer Blake Edwards
Photography Geoffrey Unsworth
Music Henry Mancini

Cast Peter Sellers, Christopher Plummer, Herbert Lom, Catherine Schell, Peter Arne, Peter Jeffrey, Gregoire Aslan, David Lodge, Graham Stark, Burt Kwouk

MURDER BY DEATH — 1976

USA Columbia — 94 mins Metro Color

Director Robert Moore
Screenplay Neil Simon

Producer Ray Stark
Photography David M. Walsh
Music David Grusin

Cast Peter Falk, Alec Guinness, Peter Sellers, Truman Capote, Estelle Winwood, Elsa Lanchester, Eileen Brennan, James Coco, David Niven, Maggie Smith, Nancy Walker

THE PINK PANTHER STRIKES AGAIN — 1976

GB United Artists/Amjo Prod. — 103 mins Panavision/De Luxe

Director Blake Edwards
Screenplay Frank Waldman and Blake Edwards

Producer Blake Edwards
Photography Harry Waxman
Music Henry Mancini

Cast Peter Sellers, Herbert Lom, Colin Blakely, Leonard Rossiter, Lesley-Anne Down, Burt Kwouk, André Maranne, Richard Vernon

REVENGE OF THE PINK PANTHER — 1978

GB United Artists/Jewel/Sellers-Edwards — 100 mins Technicolor

Director Blake Edwards
Screenplay Frank Waldman, Ron Clark, Blake Edwards

Producer Blake Edwards
Photography Ernest Day
Music Henry Mancini

Cast Peter Sellers, Dyan Cannon, Robert Webber, Burt Kwouk, Herbert Lom

THE PRISONER OF ZENDA 1979
USA Universal/Mirisch Corp 108 mins Technicolor

Director Richard Quine
Screenplay Dick Clement, Ian La Frenais (based on the novel by Anthony Hope – dramatised by Edward Rose)

Producer Walter Mirisch
Photography Arthur Ibbetson
Music Henry Mancini

Cast Peter Sellers, Lynne Frederick, Lionel Jeffries, Elke Sommer

BEING THERE 1980
USA Lorimar/North Star/C.I.P. Europaische Trehand A.G. 130 mins Metro Color/Technicolor

Director Hal Ashby
Screenplay Jerzy Kosinski (based on his novel)

Producer Andrew Braunsberg
Photography Caleb Deschanel
Music John Mandel

Cast Peter Sellers, Shirley Maclaine, Jack Warden, Melvin Douglas, Richard Dysart

THE FIENDISH PLOT OF DR FU MANCHU 1980
USA Columbia/EMI/Warner-Orion 104 mins Technicolor

Director Piers Haggard
Screenplay Jim Moloney, Rudy Dochtermaw (based on characters created by Sax Rohmer)

Producer Zev Braun and Leland Nolan
Photography Jean Tournier
Music Mark Wilkinson

Cast Peter Sellers, Helen Mirren, David Tomlinson, Steve Franken, Sid Caesar

DATE DUE

GAYLORD   PRINTED IN U.S.A.